Killie Campbell Africana Library Publications

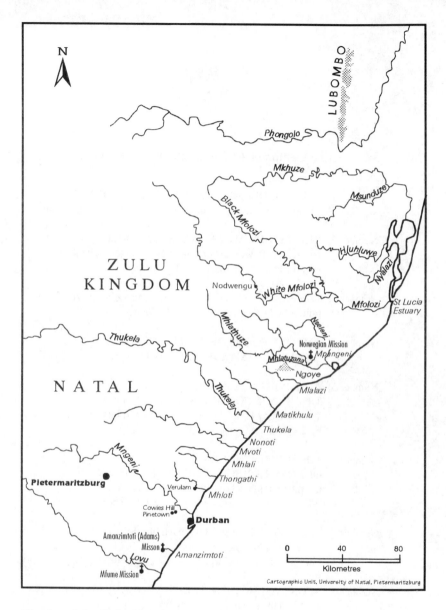

Natal and the Zulu kingdom.

The map shows features mentioned in the text but there is insufficient detail for Catherine's journey to be plotted.

CATHERINE BARTER

ALONE AMONG THE ZULUS

THE NARRATIVE OF A JOURNEY
THROUGH THE ZULU COUNTRY, SOUTH AFRICA

Edited by

PATRICIA L. MERRETT

Killie Campbell Africana Library
Durban
University of Natal Press
Pietermaritzburg
1995

ISBN 0 86980 914 8
ISBN 0 86980 529 0 (Set)

Typeset in the University of Natal Press
Pietermaritzburg
Printed by Kohler Carton and Print
Box 955, Pinetown, 3600 South Africa

CONTENTS

ILLUSTRATIONS

ACKNOWLEDGEMENTS

The map of Natal and the Zulu kingdom was specially drawn for this book by the Cartographic Unit, University of Natal, Pietermaritzburg. The picture of Sarsden House is reproduced by permission of the British Library (Add ms 36377 no. 38). The building that is reputed to have housed the school at Shipton-under-Wychwood was photographed by Patricia Merrett. All other illustrations appeared in the original edition of *Alone among the Zulus*. The cover was designed by Yvette Foord.

EDITOR'S NOTES

MISPRINTS
There are half a dozen minor misprints in the original text which have been corrected without indication.

USE OF THE TERM 'KAFIR'
Though the term 'kafir' is now unacceptable, its use in the nineteenth century was widespread and apparently generally inoffensive. It has therefore been retained in the interests of historical veracity and the integrity of the original text.

FOOTNOTES
Barter used only one footnote; this has been marked with an asterisk in its original position. To save space I have abbreviated references in my footnotes to Barter's text. Full references are given in the Select List of References.

ACKNOWLEDGEMENTS
I am indebted to Margery Moberly, University of Natal Publisher, whose idea it was to republish this book, and whose editorial advice and enthusiasm have been invaluable; to Trish Comrie for her meticulous typesetting; to Shelagh O'B. Spencer who is always generous in sharing the biographical information she has amassed; to the staffs of the University of Natal Library, Pietermaritzburg (Main and Life Sciences), and of the Killie Campbell Africana Library (especially Bobby Eldridge), for friendly assistance; to Helena Margeot of the University of Natal's Cartographic Unit for the map; to the staff of Oxfordshire County Record Office; and, above all, to my husband Christopher, whose support and encouragement made this project possible, and to whom this book is dedicated.

INTRODUCTION

Alone among the Zulus is an Englishwoman's account of a trading and hunting journey into the Zulu kingdom from April to August 1855. Catherine[1] Barter, at the age of thirty-seven, accompanied her brother Charles on this expedition. He left Catherine with the wagon, to engage in trade for cattle, while he went further north to the remote Phongolo River region to shoot elephant. Apart from a general description of the nature and hazards of travel in the region north of the Colony of Natal and of the customs of Zulu people, the major drama of her story involved her desperate struggle to rescue Charles from the threat of death from fever, possibly malaria, and from starvation. Her narrative therefore ranks as a story of travel and adventure written at a time when that genre was almost entirely male-dominated.

But this is only one aspect of the significance of *Alone among the Zulus*. It is also one of the earliest accounts of travel in the Zulu kingdom and the first known such account by a woman. Catherine Barter also wrote a novel set in Natal. She is, therefore, one of Natal's earliest literary figures. The activities and attitudes of British women in the Empire have been largely ignored and their writings have only recently begun to be studied. Their attitudes towards race, class and gender, particularly in a colonial environment, challenge aspects of nineteenth-century stereotypes of women. Their observations about colonial societies and indigenous peoples are a rich source of social history. Catherine Barter's modest, but entertaining adventure story of a hundred and forty years ago, reveals many of these facets. It is also testament to the strength of character of a woman who was acutely aware of her personal and physical plainness, but

---

1. She is commonly known as Charlotte Barter as that is the given name in the *British Museum catalogue of printed books*, but she was christened Catherine; see the Sarsden Parish Register (baptisms), Oxfordshire County Record Office and S. O'B. Spencer's *British settlers in Natal 1824–1857: a biographical register*, v.2, Pietermaritzburg, University of Natal Press, 1983, p.36. This inaccuracy probably reflects her obscurity. Her brother Charles referred to her usually as Kate and sometimes as Kitty. Friends also called her Kate; see C.A.E. Moberly, *Dulce domum: George Moberly . . .; his family and friends*, London, John Murray, 1911, pp.62 and 98.

who could be ironical about herself and who responded positively to the challenges and adventures of a remote corner of the British Empire and its neighbour, the Zulu kingdom.

*   *   *

Africa, from the British nineteenth-century perspective, was 'a man's country' and travel literature was equally a textual 'man's country'.[2] The exploits of early male travellers, hunters and missionaries such as John Barrow, R.G.G. Cumming, W. Cornwallis Harris and David Livingstone coincided with the growing interest of the British public in imperial expansion and made these men into heroic figures. The more aggressive expansion from the 1850s onwards, plus the intellectual curiosity of late Victorians, stimulated wider knowledge of anthropology and geography, empire and travel. Michelle Adler, an historian of British women travellers, has said that the 'penetration of Africa in the 1850s and 1860s acquired a narrative fascination akin to the excitement of space exploration a century later.'[3]

A significant number of British women embarked on exploration and travel in far corners of the globe, particularly in the latter half of the last century. By the end of that era, so Adler claims, a stereotype had emerged 'of an intrepid and formidable Victorian spinster, correctly − if not always comfortably − attired, vigorously prodding at distant corners of the earth with the tip of her parasol'.[4] This image is based largely on Mary Kingsley's description of how she travelled in West Africa in the 1890s; the eccentric behaviour in East Africa in the same decade of May French Sheldon − who dressed in a white ballgown and carried a ceremonial sword − reinforced that stereotype. The essentially masculine world of travel bred intense opposition to women travellers. *Punch* expressed the popular view in this well-known verse:

A lady an explorer? A traveller in skirts?
The notion's just a trifle too seraphic;
Let them stay and mind the babies, or hem our ragged shirts;
But they mustn't, can't and shan't be geographic.[5]

2. M. Adler, '"In a man's country": British women travellers in nineteenth-century South Africa', in *The societies of Southern Africa in the 19th and 20th centuries*, v. 19, London, University of London, Institute of Commonwealth Studies, 1992, p. 26.
3. Ibid.
4. Ibid., p. 27.
5. J. Trollope, *Britannia's daughters: women of the British Empire*, London, Hutchinson, 1983, p. 145. Also quoted in Adler, '"In a man's country"', p. 26.

A Royal Geographical Society member said later in the century: 'Their sex and training render them . . . unfitted for exploration . . .', and it took that august male-dominated institution over sixty years to recognise female travellers despite the wealth of botanical and anthropological information many of them brought back to Britain.[6] Although *Alone Among the Zulus* falls into the genre of travel writing and does not touch on colonial administration, it is worth noting that the same prejudice against women prevailed in the Colonial Service, which had been created to govern subject peoples. In men's memoirs of the colonial period, for instance, women are virtually invisible, while in anti-colonial novels (such as those of E. M. Forster and George Orwell) they appear as representatives of the most negative characteristics of British imperialism – its petty snobbishness, arrogance and racism.[7]

Many women travellers (and colonial women) recorded their experiences in diaries, letters, autobiography, travelogues and fiction, and these sources provide information which challenges those stereotypes. The richness of this material has been largely unmined until recently. Yet without an assessment of the role and impact of women in the British Empire through their writings, imperial history will lack a significant social dimension.[8] The republication of Catherine Barter's *Alone among the Zulus* is a move to supply that dimension.

The solitary travels of a Kingsley or a Sheldon were probably the exception; some British women certainly did travel for adventure, but many more were involuntary travellers who accompanied husbands – missionaries, colonial officials, traders, emigrants – to relatively settled and safe regions of the colonies. Others travelled to satisfy their own interests (such as painting botanical specimens, or studying indigenous peoples or engaging in missionary work on their own account), while some may have sought a marriage partner in the male-dominated colonies. Later in the century formal employment opportunities arose for those who were not economically independent or who desired meaningful work, such as nursing and teaching. Many probably left Britain to escape a society which prescribed for them a dull, obligation-filled and restricted existence: there are references by women travellers likening

6. Adler, '"In a man's country"', p. 27 and Trollope, *Britannia's daughters*, p. 145.
7. H. Callaway, *Gender, culture and empire: European women in colonial Nigeria*, Houndmills, Basingstoke, Macmillan, 1987, pp. 3 and 5–6.
8. Adler, '"In a man's country"', p. 28. See also Callaway, *Gender, culture and empire*, pp. 3–4; this is a study of how women in Nigeria, between 1900 and 1960, challenged this stereotype, and why their lives were distorted and misrepresented and they were blamed for the worst excesses of British imperialism. The period is considerably later than that of Catherine Barter, and the nature of British rule in Nigeria very different to that of settler Natal, but it offers a fascinating analysis of how the ruling male group fashioned the negative image of colonial women.

departure from Britain for foreign lands to an escape from a protected garden into a wild landscape.[9]

Despite the variety of women travellers, their writings reveal a number of common factors. They contain shared social and cultural middle class conventions and beliefs, such as high moral standards, conventional religious sentiments, instructive observations about fauna, flora and indigenous peoples, a paucity of political analysis, and emphasis on 'respectable' styles of dress, regardless of the physical surroundings.[10] But the writings can also reveal how some of these conventions were transformed by a particular colonial society, and show the different ways in which women escaped – consciously or unconsciously – the restrictions of British society.

These women travellers, products of an expanding and conquering empire, also usually shared a common perception of Africans which was couched in racial and cultural terms. Their writings also show how gender relations were maintained or transformed in a colonial environment, and how women colluded with or challenged their low status.[11]

Besides *Alone among the Zulus*, Catherine Barter also published a novel about the emigration to Natal of an English labouring couple, called *Home in South Africa* (1867). It was written to promote emigration (a concern which she shared with her brother Charles), and it is a pro-colonial moral tale of how Christian conviction and evangelical practices (self-discipline, responsibility, honesty and abstinence from alcohol), plus good luck, can enable working-class emigrants to rise in the colonial social scale. This novel also sheds light on Catherine's perceptions of class and gender roles in a colonial society as well as describing daily life in a young colony. In certain respects Catherine conformed to the late nineteenth-century popular image of a female colonial traveller, but in other respects she differed from that image, possibly because she was, in fact, a product of the early part of that century.

Another significant aspect of *Alone among the Zulus* relates to the region it covered and the date of its publication (1866). Catherine travelled at a time when European penetration of the Zulu kingdom was still in its early mercantile stages, the 1850s, and the country was still politically independent, economically self-sufficient and physically remote (or, as Catherine would have described it in typical nineteenth-century terms, still in a state of 'barbarism' and 'savagery'). So it ranks as one of the early accounts of travel, trade, and encounters with wild life and indigenous culture in the Zulu kingdom, and probably as the earliest such published record by a woman. Her novel, *Home in*

9. Adler, '"In a man's country"', pp. 28–9.
10. D. Middleton, *Victorian lady travellers*, London, Routledge & Kegan Paul, 1965, pp. 3–10.
11. Adler, '"In a man's country"', pp. 28–9.

South Africa, is also one of the first works of fiction by a woman to be set in the Colony of Natal. Apart from accounts of mission life by Mrs H. Robertson and Anne Mackenzie in the 1850s and 1860s, other better known works by Frances Ellen Colenso and Lady Barker, for instance, were published in the 1880s.[12] Catherine Barter deserves to be remembered as one of Natal's earliest woman writers. *Alone among the Zulus* was reprinted six times between 1872 and 1889 which suggests that it received considerable attention. The preface added to the 1879 printing seems to indicate that the new impression was a reflection of public interest in the Zulu engendered by the Anglo-Zulu War.[13]

At a personal level, these books also reveal a woman of austere character and behaviour, highly literate, with strong religious and educational ambitions and the independence to carry them out, and with courage and physical stamina. But she was an obscure figure in Natal colonial society, for a number of reasons. She seems to have been a very private person. In the opening paragraph of *Alone among the Zulus* she describes herself emphatically as physically plain, blunt of speech and simple in her dress. Clearly she was very conscious of her blunt manner and undistinguished looks (which may explain why no photograph of her has been located). Perhaps her early nineteenth-century education had stressed women's decorative function in society, or perhaps she contrasted unfavourably with certain members of her family; we know, for instance that her brother Charles was a convivial spirit,[14] that her uncle Robert Speckott Barter (Warden at Winchester College) was a warm-hearted and popular figure, and that her grandmother was described as having a beautiful and cheerful nature.[15]

---

12. *Home in South Africa* was also published by the S.P.C.K., in 1867, and under the pseudonym 'By a plain woman.' One of the earliest non-fiction works was Eliza Feilden's *My African home; or, Bush life in Natal when a young colony (1852–7)*, but this was first published in 1887, by Sampson Low, in London (reprinted by Griggs, Durban, 1973). Mrs H. Robertson wrote in *The mission field*, in 1856, 1862 and 1864, and Anne Mackenzie wrote two short books, in 1857 and 1860 (both published by R. Grant, Edinburgh). Other non-fiction works, by Frances Ellen Colenso, Lady Barker, Mrs A. M. Wilkinson, and Lady Florence Dixie were all published in the 1880s. Fiction is even more scarce: F.E. Colenso wrote a short story in the *Natal Colonist* (date unknown) which was reprinted by Davis & Sons in 1876 in Durban, a decade after Catherine's novel appeared. For an assessment of Frances Colenso's place in South Africa's literary history see the Introduction to her *My Chief and I, or, six months in Natal after the Langalibalele outbreak, (originally published under the pseudonym Atherton Wylde), and Five Years later; a sequel*, edited and introduced by M.J. Daymond, Pietermaritzburg, University of Natal Press, 1994.
13. See *A South African bibliography to the year 1925*: being a revision and continuation of Sydney Mendelssohn's South African bibliography, 1910, edited at the South African Library, v. 1, London, Mansell, 1979, p. 144.
14. Hattersley records him entertaining the Pietermaritzburg agricultural show diners to 'rollicking choruses'. See *Pietermaritzburg panorama*, Pietermaritzburg, Shuter and Shooter, 1938, p. 84.
15. Moberly, *Dulce domum*, pp. 60–1; A.F. Hattersley, '"Oxford collegian": Charles Barter', in *Oliver the spy, and others: a little gallery of South African portraits*, Cape Town, Maskew Miller, 1959, p. 108.

Catherine's style of dress (at least in Natal), appears to have been rather quaint: a Natal contemporary wrote that she dressed 'in the style of a sisterhood, in a close bonnet, with small white linen collar and cuffs on her black silk dress of a peculiar shape'.[16] In the Zulu country Catherine described her cap as having 'a plain quilling of net round the face . . .'[17] Like that of most of her contemporaries, this dress was not entirely suitable for the extremes of climate nor for the physical demands of travel in a wagon, but she clung to it as a sign of respectability (a value shared by other Victorian women), and as a mark of her commitment to a particular lifestyle.

Apart from passing references to Catherine during the eight months of Charles's Natal diary,[18] which reveal her social acquaintances, domestic duties and religious and mission activities, there are few contemporary references to Catherine and those which have survived are brief. Apart from comments on her dress, she is described as a devoted missionary and teacher who quickly mastered the Zulu language. According to Bishop Colenso (and his account is confirmed by Charles's diary[19]), in the 1850s she gave catechism lessons on Sunday afternoons to African servants in Pietermaritzburg, by whom she was known at first as 'the great white elephant' (referring to her dignity) and later as No-musa or 'mother of mercy'.[20] Mrs Eliza Feilden records her as walking to African kraals in the sub-tropical heat of Natal's coastal region to proselytise, as being prepared to sleep on an African mat on the ground, and as enduring 'various voluntary privations'.[21] Catherine also eschewed a public persona; both her books were published anonymously – by 'A Plain Woman' – an early nineteenth-century convention for women writers. But Natalians learnt of her role in rescuing Charles from certain death – reports of the disastrous trip preceded their return – and Piet Hogg, hunter and trader, recorded many years later her bravery in that adventure.[22]

Catherine only spent about 26 of her 77 years in Natal (1852–5; 1857–1864; and early 1880s to her death in 1895); the other 50 years she lived in England. She appears to have lived in Oxfordshire (her home county) from 1864 to the early 1880s. During this period she was supervising the education of Salome Welayo, the daughter of a Zulu man whom she had converted to Christianity on

16. Feilden, *My African home*, pp. 119–20.
17. *Alone among the Zulus*, p. 33.
18. C. Rickard 'Charles Barter, Natal diary, 14 August 1852 – 26 April 1853', edited with an introductory essay, place and personality index, B.A. Honours essay, University of Natal, Pietermaritzburg, 1975. The original is in the Killie Campbell Africana Library, Durban.
19. Ibid., p. 48.
20. J. W. Colenso, *Ten weeks in Natal: a journal of a first tour of visitation among the colonists and Zulu kafirs of Natal*, Cambridge, Macmillan, 1855, pp. 49–50.
21. Feilden, *My African home*, pp. 119–20 and 265.
22. Piet Hogg's 'Reminiscences', Kit Bird Collection, v. 7, Natal Archives, p. 40.

her brother Charles's farm. This seems to have been the closest she came to carrying out her ambition to buy African children from their parents, to educate them and to return them to their families at sixteen years so that they could teach and influence them.[23] (From the evidence of *Alone among the Zulus* it appears that she had on an earlier occasion cared for and probably educated a young Zulu child who had been rescued from death in the Thukela River after the battle of Ndondakusuka in 1856.[24])

Catherine opened a small boarding school in Shipton-under-Wychwood[25] and ensured that Salome emerged with the accomplishments of a Victorian young woman: she could play the piano and speak French; she could not speak Zulu. Salome later married an Englishman in Pietermaritzburg and she and her husband lived on Catherine's property 'Wychwood'. But this experiment in cultural adaptation did not succeed in racist colonial Natal; the couple were ostracised and the marriage seems to have broken up, probably after Catherine's death. Some time after Catherine died, Salome went back to England and to an unknown fate.[26] This experiment in acculturation must have given some satisfaction to Catherine as it proved her belief that Africans had the potential to absorb English culture and education and to adopt a middle class lifestyle. In this respect she differed from many Natal colonists who saw Africans simply as a potential proletariat. It also indicates her commitment to the missionary ideal and to education for girls. It may also reveal an awareness that her experiment would not succeed in colonial society; she had a low opinion of the general educational level of most colonists and could not have approved of the extreme racism exhibited by many of them. But little is known about these years in her life.

Before looking more closely at the questions raised so far – to what extent Catherine's writing conformed to the common features of British women writers (particularly with regard to gender, race and class), what they reveal about the Zulu kingdom, and why her lifestyle took its particular contours – the following section will discuss her early nineteenth-century religious, social and educational context, which help explain Catherine's attitudes and way of life.

* * *

23. Feilden, *My African home*, p. 120.
24. *Alone among the Zulus*, p. 21. See also p. 21, note 14 where this child's rescue and upbringing are discussed.
25. This was a village quite near Sarsden (where she grew up) and where her brother Henry was vicar from 1868–1900 (see list of rectors hanging in St. Mary the Virgin Church). The archivist of the Shipton-under-Wychwood Local History Society identified this school and adjacent house for Shelagh O'Byrne Spencer. In 1871 there were 11 pupils, 2 teachers, a cook and a housemaid plus Catherine. See Spencer, *British settlers in Natal*, v. 2, p. 37.
26. See Spencer, *British settlers in Natal*, v. 2, pp. 37–8.

Catherine Barter was born in 1818 the eldest of nine siblings,[27] into a family of rural, country clergy, of a 'good' family with ample means. This meant, in material terms, that the Barters possessed their own carriage, employed at least a butler, a maid and a nurse, as well as a bailiff to manage the property attached to the parish church. Her grandfather was educated at Tiverton and Balliol College, Oxford, and served as curate and then rector to Cornworthy in Devon. He kept harriers and in later life composed 'graceful verse'.[28] The conjunction of an elite education, the profession of clergyman, and an interest in hunting and literary composition were hallmarks of the Barter family. Catherine's father, the Revd Charles Barter (c. 1786–1868) was rector of the rural parish of Sarsden and the adjacent village of Churchill in Oxfordshire, in the eastern Cotswolds. Her mother was Elizabeth Catherine Langston, sister of the squire of Sarsden (James Haughton Langston, 1796–1863) to whom the Revd Charles often acted as clerk.[29] Two of her uncles (Robert Speckott and William Brudenell) and one brother, Henry, were also clergymen. This preponderance of clergy in the family, and the importance of religion to Catherine, were common phenomena in nineteenth-century England.

The Anglican Church was the established church, and legal restrictions on other denominations meant that Anglicans dominated all public institutions; the majority of the landed gentry were Anglican. But the obverse side of this privileged position was state control of many aspects of the Church's life and the expectation that the Church would serve the state and uphold its authority. The parish clergyman not only ministered to his parishioners' spiritual needs; he was also expected to teach them, influence their social behaviour, and inculcate deference to their superiors and loyalty to the state.[30] The Anglican clergy have been called 'the spiritual wing of the dominant class'.[31]

A Church so subservient to the state and the aristocracy inevitably suffered a decline in its religious life, and increasingly the Anglican Church lost touch with people in the countryside and in the towns. Pluralism, absenteeism and

27. Eleven children were born but one died at the age of 14 months. Their baptismal dates and names were: Catherine 1818; Charles 1820; Elizabeth 1821; Mary 1825; Jane 1827; James 1829 (buried 1830); Ellen 1830; William 1832; Henrietta 1834; Henry 1836; and George 1839. See the list of baptisms in the Sarsden Parish Register, Oxfordshire County Record Office.
28. Hattersley, '"Oxford collegian": Charles Barter', pp. 103–4.
29. Charles's marriage to Elizabeth Catherine Langston in 1817 is recorded in the Sarsden Parish Register, Oxfordshire County Record Office. Elizabeth Langston's relationship to the local squire is recorded in the dedication below the north-east window of All Saints' Church, Churchill, Oxfordshire. See also pamphlet 'All Saints' Church, Churchill', issued 1984. The personal names index in the Oxfordshire C.R.O. records Charles's duties as clerk to Langston.
30. J. Obelkevich, 'Religion' in *The Cambridge social history of Britain 1750–1950*, v.3, ed. by F.M.L. Thompson, Cambridge, University Press, 1990, p.312.
31. J. Guy, *The heretic: a study of the life of John William Colenso 1814–1883*, Pietermaritzburg, University of Natal Press, 1983, p.183.

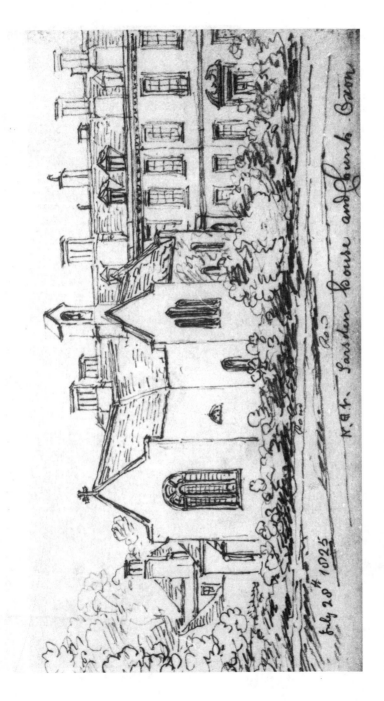

Side view of Sarsden House showing the chapel.　　　By permission of The British Library (Add ms 36377 no. 38)

The school Catherine founded at Shipton-under-Wychwood is reputed to have been located in these houses facing the village green.

P. Merrett, September 1994

careerism were rife: by 1830 only 40 per cent of the parishes were served by resident incumbents, and this 'creaking, unreformed machinery was both a handicap and a public scandal'.[32] Alienation from the Anglican Church was increased by the expansion of the class of gentlemen clergy, men with private incomes or with substantial livings, who lived in luxurious parsonages and affected an upper class lifestyle. About one in five clergymen sat on the bench by the 1820s and therefore acted as the arm of a repressive government.[33] By the early nineteenth-century the Anglican Church to which the Barter family belonged was being seriously challenged by Methodism and the dissenting sects.

The Revd Charles Barter was one of the resident parsons, but he was also a gentleman cleric, which is to say that he participated in the leisure pursuits of the Oxfordshire gentry, that is, riding to hounds and shooting pheasants. The Game Act of 1831 entitled tenants of land, and not only landowners, to kill game, and the Revd Barter took out licences for this purpose. As Hattersley has observed, 'in a hunting country, a parson who ignored the field counted for little in his pulpit'.[34] Perhaps it was the more incumbent on Barter to socialise with the local gentry because, unlike many rural rectors, he did not act as a local government functionary, although he did apparently carry out some of the functions of the local squire Langston (his brother-in-law) when the latter was absent.[35] The village squire traditionally acted as the local justice of the peace and carried out all rural government functions (operation of the poor law; commanding the local volunteer yeomanry, and so on).

The Barter family seem generally to have been 'high' church, that is, in favour of traditional Anglican ritual. The Revd Charles Barter later in life acted as an advisor to Bishop Samuel Wilberforce (Bishop of Oxford from 1845). When the latter was accused, in 1859, of sympathy with the Church of Rome, Charles Barter defended him. He nevertheless remained essentially a country gentleman 'free from all extremes of doctrine and ritual'.[36] His brother Robert Speckott Barter, who was Warden at Winchester College, was later described by a contemporary as a staunch churchman 'of the old school'; he also socialised with high churchmen such as Bishop Wilberforce.[37] Robert was a friend of the headmaster of Winchester College, George Moberly (who was a more liberal individual), but he apparently did not sympathise with Moberly's close friendship with his neighbour, Dr John Keble, one of the leaders of the Oxford Movement which emphasised the Catholic origins and ritual of the

32. Obelkevich, 'Religion', pp. 312–13.
33. Ibid., p. 313.
34. Hattersley, ' "Oxford collegian": Charles Barter', p. 104.
35. Ibid.
36. Ibid., p. 105.
37. Moberly, *Dulce domum*, pp. 62 and 66–7.

Anglican Church.[38] At least two of the Revd Charles's sons (Charles and Henry) were educated at the traditionally Anglican Oxford University. Charles – who was certainly a Tory politically and socially – has been described as a conservative high churchman.[39] It is probably safe to assume that Catherine also was a conventional Anglican with all this implied in terms of conservative social and political ideas. Both Catherine and Charles were friends of Bishop Colenso in Natal, at least until the early 1860s when Colenso's controversial and enlightened theological writings led to his being deposed on a charge of heresy and the Church of England in South Africa splitting into two warring factions. Charles was thereafter more closely associated with Dean Green, a bitter opponent of the Bishop.[40]

By the turn of the eighteenth century, however, all Christian sects – and indeed many levels of society – had been deeply influenced by evangelicalism, that powerful eighteenth century reaction against the worldliness which had crept into Anglican faith and practice. At the beginning of the nineteenth century about one tenth of the Anglican clergy were evangelicals, as were many lay Anglicans. Obelkevich has pointed out that in the pre-1815 period when England was embroiled in wars and felt threatened by revolutionary France, evangelicalism came to hold a special moral significance:

> To Britain evangelicals offered what has been called a 'new moral economy' of sobriety, self-control, sexual restraint and respectability; a challenge both to the hedonism of the aristocracy and to the levelling and violence of the Revolution, it inaugurated that 'Victorianism' which appeared decades before the accession of Queen Victoria herself.[41]

38. Ibid., p. 153.
39. Rickard, 'Charles Barter, Natal diary', p. 1.
40. There is evidence of friendship between the Barters and the Colensos in the 1850s. In December 1855, when Catherine returned to Britain, she accompanied a governess imported by the Colensos, who was sent home due to mental illness. Apparently this woman involved Catherine in a public fracas in Durban which resulted in Catherine being unfairly summonsed on a charge of assault. See Feilden, *My African home*, p. 265. For a few months in 1856 Charles edited the *Natal Guardian*, which promoted High Church Anglicanism and which was believed to have Bishop Colenso's support or involvement, although Charles denied this. In that year the Bishop married Charles to his second wife, Emma Henrietta Arabella Butler, one of the Bishop's missionary assistants. See Rickard, 'Charles Barter, Natal diary', pp. 18–19; Hattersley, ' "Oxford collegian": Charles Barter', p. 124; and Spencer, *British settlers in Natal*, v. 3, p. 104. Charles' ignominious involvement in the Bushman's River Pass affair during the 1873 Langalibalele 'rebellion' was viewed with scorn by the Colensos; see W. Rees, ed., *Colenso letters from Natal*, Pietermaritzburg, Shuter and Shooter, 1958, p. 276, and two letters from Bishop Colenso to Major Durnford, 10 November 1873 and 27 November 1873, in the Natal Archives, Faye Papers, A131, Box 14. I am indebted to Shelagh Spencer for the last two references.
41. Obelkevich, 'Religion', p. 326.

Evangelicalism gained most support from the middle classes because its social message suited them and gave them the means to distinguish themselves from the idle rich and the rude lower orders. This creed condemned idleness and advocated hard work, moral rectitude, and the belief that the social order was God-given. It was a conservative ethos and Anglican evangelicals, as a minority strand within the Church, were typically socially and politically conservative. Their religious creed was essentially fundamentalist, deeply introspective and judgmental. Evangelicals believed in the Bible as the literal Word of God, in salvation by faith (and only for the elect), and had a powerful sense of original sin, and the threat of eternal damnation. They advocated scrutiny of the morality of every action and strict Sabbatarianism, and had a strong motivation to evangelise and missionise. Thus service and action, rather than creed, were stressed, and prayer, Bible-reading and good works became characteristic evangelical – and middle class – activities.[42] Some of these practices are evident in Catherine's life, particularly the philanthropy and charity.

Victorian charity gave Britain a philanthropic tradition unrivalled by any other European country. Victorian philanthropists worked energetically to care for the poor and sick through visits, nursing and distribution of food and clothing, and extended their charity to virtually every downtrodden class and institution in society. These included ragged schools, Sunday Schools for the poor, and overseas missions. Foreign missions were early and popular charities, as the establishment in the 1790s of the Church Missionary Society and the Religious Tract Society proves; in 1804 the British and Foreign Bible Society was founded. The English seemed to distinguish little between foreign and domestic missions. Philanthropic activities were so extensive and so common that they have been described as an informal, unsystematic 'apparatus of social services'. They were motivated largely by a conservative impulse: to uphold the family as the basic unit of British society, and to transmit to the lower orders (whether British working class or colonial 'savages') the values of middle class British family life, especially the virtues of self-help.[43]

Missionary and philanthropic activities thus operated at a number of levels: they can be seen as a means of social control and imperialism, they offered a means to personal salvation, they satisfied basic humanitarian instincts.[44] Finally such activities were also significant in the role and status of middle class Victorian women. In gender terms, evangelical philanthropy had the contradic-

---

42. Ibid., pp. 321–3.
43. F. K. Prochaska, 'Philanthropy', in *The Cambridge social history of Britain 1750–1950*, v. 3, pp. 357–8, 360–1 and 367; F. M. L. Thompson, *The rise of respectable society: a social history of Victorian Britain 1830–1900*, London, Fontana, 1988, p. 252; and A. Wood, *Nineteenth century Britain 1815–1914*, 2nd ed., London, Longman, 1982, p. 24.
44. Prochaska, 'Philanthropy', pp. 360–2, 370–2 and 377–9.

tory effects of reinforcing patriarchal authority (through the popular custom of the father conducting daily prayers for the whole household), and widening women's spheres of activity by sanctioning philanthropy outside the home. As F.M.L. Thompson has said, it freed women from 'a purdah of antimacassars and domesticity' and in many instances put women in touch with social groups beyond their menfolk.[45]

When speculating as to the origins of Catherine's dedication to missionary work, one can perhaps search for other social and economic influences apart from Anglicanism, evangelicalism and philanthropy. For instance, the 1820s and 30s were generally a period of cyclical harvest failures and industrial boom and slump, and these caused considerable social unrest. It was also a period of radical working class activism. The labourers' revolt of 1830 (in response to bad harvests and a severe winter) started in the southern counties of Hampshire and Wiltshire, which were seriously affected, and spread northwards; Oxfordshire was also affected, but less widely. The riots were repressed but they caused great alarm amongst landowners.[46] These events occurred when Catherine was eleven years old and may well have aroused the Barter family's anxiety about 'the lower orders' and further stimulated the missionary impulse. The Chartist riots of the late 1830s and early 40s, which were also suppressed by the military, further stoked class antagonisms and middle class fears of revolution. In addition, the social and economic distress of these early years placed a heavy burden on poor relief, which was administered in the counties by the local squires, and given the social proximity of the Barters to the Langston family, must have been known to them. As early as the 1820s some parish authorities began assisting families to emigrate to the colonies, and local associations sprang up for the same purpose, in which contributing landlords and clergymen could nominate prospective emigrants. Between 1836 and 1846 they assisted over 14 000 people to emigrate.[47] This process may also have influenced Charles and Catherine in their interest in Natal and in emigration, and Catherine in her sensitivity to the less privileged. Being literate and educated, the Barters were probably also aware of current 'condition of England' debates and socially conscious literature such as Disraeli's novel *Sybil* (published in 1845), which coined the famous phrase 'the two nations' to describe the unbridgeable gulf between the British poor and the well-to-do classes.

45. Thompson, *The rise of respectable society*, p. 253; see also Obelkevich, 'Religion', pp. 320 and 341.
46. Wood, *Nineteenth century Britain*, p. 78; P. Horn, *The rural world 1780–1850: social change in the English countryside*, London, Hutchinson, 1980, pp. 91–3.
47. W. A. Armstrong, 'The countryside', in *The Cambridge social history of Britain 1750–1950*, v. 1, p. 105.

Given this background, Catherine's activities and attitudes are hardly surprising: her strict Sabbatarianism, her Sunday school teaching, her visiting the poor and sick,[48] her Sunday reading of prayers and the Bible to her African driver while on the journey through the Zulu kingdom, and her interest in education (which is evident both in her didactic tone in the first chapter of her travel book, in the passing reference to something she once heard in an English 'national school of a country village',[49] and in her 'adoption' and educating of Salome), her serious and service-oriented lifestyle and dress, and her essentially conservative ethic of empire which viewed the Zulu kingdom as a fit area of settlement and civilising for the British. Charles, by contrast, did not share his older sister's solemn lifestyle, but he too was a regular church goer and was actively involved in church affairs.[50] He also seems to have supported Catherine in her missionary activities.

As the clerical family serving both Sarsden and the adjacent parish of Churchill, the Barters would have been members of the 'agricultural interest'. Oxfordshire society followed the general tripartite structure of English county society – aristocracy and gentry at the top (village squires, such as James Haughton Langston at Sarsden occupied the lowest ranks of this upper class), wealthy tenant farmers in the middle, and landless labourers at the bottom. But the social and other services rendered by tradespeople, craftsmen and the clergy in villages and county towns were also part of that structure. By virtue of the tithe (paid by all farmers in the parish regardless of denomination), the clergy were partly supported by the agricultural sector.[51] The Revd Charles Barter, due to his family connections with the gentry and his occasional deputising for Langston, linked the Barters to the agricultural interest and raised their social status. It appears that the only ecclesiastical building in rural Sarsden (which has no village) was the chapel attached to Sarsden House, and it was probably here that all the Barter children were baptised. This background probably inculcated in the Barters conservative social and political beliefs based on veneration for landed property and the status quo, and consistent with their High Church affiliations.[52]

---

48. See Rickard, 'Charles Barter, Natal diary', pp. 40 and 56, where Charles records Catherine visiting women who were either ill or had recently given birth.
49. *Alone among the Zulus*, p. 3.
50. When the local chapel at Karkloof was purchased by the Anglicans, both Charles and Dean Green were made trustees of the property until a new Bishop was consecrated. See *Times of Natal*, 12 September 1866. I am indebted to Shelagh Spencer for this reference.
51. Armstrong, 'The countryside', pp. 89–94.
52. The deep commitment of at least one member of the Barter family, viz. the Revd Henry, to the landed interest, emerges in an account of an agricultural strike in 1873 in the parish of Shipton-under-Wychwood. The clerical magistrates of that parish (and of another local parish), i.e. the vicars, committed 16 women (including 2 with babies in arms) to a week's hard

The pre-eminent leisure pursuit of the gentry was fox-hunting, followed closely by other field sports. By the 1840s fox-hunting had developed into a ritualistic and exclusive cult which was aspired to by any *nouveau riche*; this may explain Charles Barter's social snobbery, his landed lifestyle in Natal, and his obsession with hunting and dogs.[53] Catherine was also a horsewoman. Although we cannot be absolutely sure where she lived before emigrating to Natal, she seems to have chosen to live most of her life either in or near villages – either in Oxfordshire or colonial Natal (Pietermaritzburg was nothing more than an agricultural village in the 1850s, and she died on her own property 'Wychwood', some kilometres from Pietermaritzburg.)

The Barters' rural lifestyle was probably more typical of the English middle classes than that of, say middle class Londoners, for even into the 1840s England was a largely rural society. Although by the 1850s the majority of people were urbanised, most towns – except for seven large towns – were merely large villages where the rhythm of life was still tied to the land. Furthermore, in the 1820s and 30s, when Catherine was growing up, coaches and horses were the common means of transport. Rural people were therefore quite isolated. Only that small fraction of the population living in large towns, which was the 'advanced guard of modern urban society', as F.M.L. Thompson observes, experienced acutely the rapid social change, the social problems, and the new lifestyles and customs which are now seen as characteristic of the Victorian age.[54] Those educated people who lived largely in the counties – such as the Barters – while being aware of the problems of industrial urban life, succeeded in avoiding their direct experience.

The Barters had connections with educated clerical society in the southern counties: the Barter grandparents lived in Devon, uncle William Brudenell Barter was in the 1830s Rector at Burghclere, Hampshire which lies about 30kms north of Winchester, and there was the connection with Winchester College where Catherine's uncle Robert Speckott Barter was Warden (responsible for discipline and welfare of the scholars).[55] The young Barters became friends with the family of Dr G. Moberly, Headmaster of Winchester and from

---

labour, and were criticised by the Home Secretary for that decision. Henry was appointed vicar of Shipton-under-Wychwood in 1868, and was presumably therefore one of the responsible clerics. See B. Smith, *The Cotswolds*, Stroud, Allan Sutton, 1992, pp. 93–4.

53. See J.F.C. Harrison, *The early Victorians 1832–1851*, London, Weidenfeld and Nicolson, 1971, pp. 92–4; and a reading of Charles's diary which reveals his great interest in horses and hunting. See also Rickard's comments in her 'Charles Barter, Natal diary', pp. 15 and 25, and Hattersley, '"Oxford collegian": Charles Barter', pp. 105–6 and 118–19.

54. In 1831 there were only seven towns (including London, Birmingham and Liverpool) with a population over 100 000 inhabitants, and they only contained about one sixth of the total British population. See Thompson, *The rise of respectable society*, pp. 26–8.

55. Moberly, *Dolce domum*, p. 60; and Hattersley, '"Oxford collegian": Charles Barter', p. 108.

1869 Bishop of Salisbury, and one of his daughters was to marry Henry Barter. According to a Moberly family memoir, when grandfather Barter died in the 1840s, grandmother Barter went to live with Robert in Winchester and she had her granddaughters from Sarsden 'constantly with her, especially Kate and Lizzie Barter . . .' (probably Catherine's younger sister Elizabeth Barter, baptised 1821) whom she calls 'clever, eager people, who made great friends with us.'[56] It was on the occasion of the Moberlys' move to a new brick house in Winchester in 1841 that Catherine wrote a poem which is quoted here because it reveals her evangelical upbringing as well as her literary abilities:

'Tis true our walls are unadorned,
Though strongly built and fair;
But mark their deep foundations laid
With curious art and care.

E'en such the pride of Wykeham's race,
Not in vain wit displayed;
But solid learning on the base
Of true religion laid.[57]

Catherine was acquainted with Charlotte M. Yonge, the popular Victorian novelist, who was a friend of the Moberlys, and when Warden Barter dined with the Moberlys, Wordsworth and English poetry were discussed. Both Warden Barter and Dr Moberly entertained widely, the former's house being always open to Wykehamists and the latter entertaining a wide group of people drawn from 'Cathedral, College, Barracks and the Town'.[58] One of the masters at Winchester, for instance, from 1835 to 1846, was Charles Wordsworth (nephew of the poet and later Bishop of St. Andrews); he was very close to Warden Barter, and in 1846 married William Brudenell Barter's daughter Katharine.[59] In a memoir of one of the Moberly daughters, who was considerably younger than Catherine, it is apparent that the Moberly family life was a cultured and social one.[60]

Upbringing amongst the upper middle classes in the early nineteenth-century was strict and regimented, and children were supervised by nannies, maids and governesses. (We know that the Barter parents employed a nurse for their

---

56. Moberly, *Dulce domum*, pp. 61–2.
57. Ibid., p. 72.
58. Ibid., p. 160; see also pp. 66 and 98.
59. C. Wordsworth, *Annals of my early life 1806–1846*, London, Longmans, Green, 1891, pp. 170, 289 and 314.
60. E. Olivier, *Four Victorian ladies of Wiltshire*, London, Faber, 1945, chapter on 'Miss Annie Moberly'.

children.) The aim was to produce responsible and respectable adults, and the values rigorously instilled were discipline, obedience, honesty, cleanliness, humility and unremitting charity to others. Children's recreation was carefully supervised for its moral content and gender bias.[61] Overarching all these activities and values were of course religion and religious practices. This austere picture does not necessarily mean that all early nineteenth-century children were brought up in the inflexible style which is now considered typical of the Victorian family. F.M.L. Thompson claims that it is not an accurate description of middle class culture – not even in the heyday of the Victorian age – except possibly for early Quaker homes where domestic culture was 'plain in speech and dress and shorn of all frivolity, ornament or display'.[62] Thompson's words conjure up immediately Catherine's opening words to her book *Alone among the Zulus* – where she stresses her plainness – and it would seem that she consciously chose a lifestyle with Quaker overtones. According to Thompson, the austere tone of puritanical-evangelical propaganda is indicative of the fact that most Victorians were unregenerate samplers of worldly pleasures (modest and morally approved though they were), than of the success of this narrow social creed.[63]

Catherine does seem to have acquired a high sense of sisterly duty to her younger brother Charles, since she was prepared to accompany him to the undeveloped Colony of Natal and care for him in his bachelor state. Although this is consistent with nineteenth-century beliefs about the role of women, there seems to have been genuine affection between brother and sister and it is unclear whether affection or duty weighed more heavily with Catherine when deciding her future. Perhaps there was also ambition; Catherine may have been a victim of the narrow role envisaged for women in early nineteenth-century England, and it may have been to escape these limitations that she chose to go to the colonies, where she would have scope to fulfil her missionary ambitions. Once her brother was married and she had embarked on her experiment to educate an African child, she returned to England and set up a boarding school.

There were no state-run schools in England in this era of *laissez-faire* policies, but the sons of the upper middle classes had opportunities to gain an elite education. Catherine's brothers Charles and Henry went to Winchester and Eton respectively and both attended Oxford. Little is known about Catherine's formal education except that at some stage (according to a chance remark in her brother's Natal diary) she attended a school in Lyneham.[64] Nothing is known of

---

61. Thompson, *The rise of respectable society*, pp. 125–7.
62. Ibid., p. 254.
63. Ibid., pp. 256–7.
64. Rickard, 'Charles Barter, Natal diary', p. 34. There are three Lynehams, all small hamlets: near Sarsden in Oxfordshire; near Swindon in Wiltshire; and in Devon. Charles Barter hunted on

this school; presumably it was a small private or proprietorial institution and as in the case of many such schools, there would be no surviving records.[65] Her writings reveal that she was highly literate, well-informed and musical – and this was not unusual for the children of upper middle class families in the early nineteenth century; her contemporaries Florence Nightingale and George Eliot for instance both had received a good education as did many daughters in Unitarian, Quaker or radical families. One of the Moberly daughters who had no formal education at all gave herself a liberal education based on her father's library, taught herself Greek and Hebrew, and in the 1880s was invited to become principal of a women's college in Oxford.[66] It is likely that Catherine's education was oriented towards literature and languages, and of course religion, and that the underlying values were the middle class evangelical ones discussed above. She also travelled abroad at least once; between late 1851 and March 1852 Catherine was living in France with Charles; they did some travelling and he wrote up the account of his recent exploratory trip to Natal called *The dorp and the veld; or, six months in Natal* (London, Orr, 1852). Why they went to France at that time is unknown.

*   *   *

Since the impulse to emigrate to the Natal Colony probably originated with Charles Barter, it is worth considering his motives. Charles claimed to have an interest in fostering emigration to the British colonies. He took himself off to Canada (to the forests of New Brunswick) and then to the United States of America where he lived and worked for three years. When he returned to England in 1849, the country was in a deep economic depression, and the only occupations apparently open to him were the Church or academia. As neither appealed to him, he became interested in the Colony of Natal: the Byrne emigration scheme to Natal was then being publicised. He also appears to have been impressed by the South African exploits of the famous hunter R. Gordon Cumming. Charles spent the period September 1850 to June 1851 in Natal and the interior, and by March 1852, after reconsidering and rejecting Canada, he and Catherine decided to emigrate to Natal and take a working class family with

Dartmoor with a companion who came from the latter Lyneham (see Hattersley, '"Oxford collegian": Charles Barter', p. 105).

65. G. Sutherland, 'Education', in *The Cambridge social history of Britain 1750–1950*, v. 3, p. 132.
66. Olivier, *Four Victorian ladies of Wiltshire*, p. 31.

them. Charles's account of his experiences in South Africa, *The dorp and the veld*, was written ostensibly to encourage possible emigrants.[67]

The Natal Colony in the 1840s was an undeveloped and economically valueless corner of the British Empire. It had been settled by a small group of hunter-trader Europeans from the Cape Colony as recently as 1824, and had been annexed as a district of the Cape Colony in 1844, for purely strategic reasons. The only source of income was the export of raw commodities – until the 1860s mainly ivory, skins and hides – and thereafter wool and sugar. Until the 1860s Natal was dependent on the Cape Colony for the forwarding of manufactured goods, for which it had to pay double duties. What altered Natal's prospects was the immigration, between 1849 and 1852, of nearly 5 000 settlers, mostly from Britain, but a few from western Europe and the British Colony of Mauritius. These last were to establish Natal's coastal sugar industry; the bulk of British settlers engaged in trade and Natal was soon covered by a commercial network and a sprinkling of villages. But the Colony remained highly vulnerable to fluctuations in the international economy.[68]

Pietermaritzburg, where the Barters settled, became a commercial centre but remained an agricultural village. The 1852 census revealed a population of 2 400, of whom 1 508 were Europeans. Out of 104 respondents in 1854, 50 householders described themselves as farmers, the rest being engaged in commerce. The clay and sod walled cottages were gradually being replaced by brick, and thatch and tile roofs were beginning to be replaced by the new galvanised iron. But the wide streets were unpaved, and there was no lighting. In the dry winters, the town was enveloped in dust storms, and in the summer rains the roads were impassable except for ox-wagons. Social amenities were still scarce; the first hotel had only been opened in 1849 and the garrison supplied the main entertainments. After the first elections were held for limited representative government in 1857, the legislature met in the government schoolroom, a large thatched barn-like building.[69]

Charles had not been impressed by Pietermaritzburg on his exploratory visit

---

67. Hattersley, '"Oxford collegian": Charles Barter', pp. 110–17. See also Rickard, 'Charles Barter, Natal diary', pp. 2–3, and Barter, *The dorp and the veld*, (London, Orr, 1852) p. 45 where he mentions Cumming's exhibition.
68. C. Ballard, 'Traders, trekkers and colonists', in A. Duminy and B. Guest, eds, *Natal and Zululand from earliest times to 1910: a new history*, Pietermaritzburg, University of Natal Press, 1989, pp. 123–9 and 137–8.
69. For a general description of Pietermaritzburg in the 1840s and early 1850s, see Hattersley, *Pietermaritzburg panorama*, pp. 24–43. One of his sources is Charles Barter's *The dorp and the veld*.

in 1850–1,[70] but he was familiar with colonial life after his experiences in Canada and his exploratory trip to Natal. It must, however, have been a novel experience for Catherine, despite her familiarity with English rural and village life.

A prominent feature of Natal settler society was its racism. Charles Barter shared these opinions: in *The dorp and the veld* he had recommended the extermination of the Bushmen and had condemned the role of British philanthropists in the eastern Cape frontier wars. The belief in racial equality he called 'at best an amiable theory, unsupported by a single evidence drawn from sound reason or experience.'[71] But Catherine's values and attitudes towards race were more complex and certainly less crude than her brother's. Her racial attitudes, and her perception of the African landscape form an interesting comparison and contrast with those of Harriet Ward, an emigrant to the eastern Cape in the early 1840s, who wrote two books, one about her experiences entitled *Five years in kaffirland* (1848) and a novel called *Jasper Lyle: a tale of kaffirland* (1852).

Two major influences in British society underpinned settler attitudes to Africans. One was a belief in the great chain of being, which had been fixed at creation and which stretched from the highest form of life (white, Anglo-Saxon) down to the lowest form of human life (black people). (It was only after Darwin's *Origin of species*, published in 1859, that this notion began slowly to be challenged.) The second influence was the evangelical belief that 'natural man' was brutish and unregenerate, lacking shame and a moral sense. For one group of Victorians, these beliefs justified the harsh treatment meted out to indigenous peoples in British colonies, but to another, evangelicalism taught that 'savage' peoples had to be civilised and christianized to save them from hell.[72] Harriet Ward seems to have fallen into the former category while Catherine belonged to the latter.

Harriet (born 1808) accompanied her officer husband to the eastern Cape frontier, which was in 1842 embroiled in conflict with the Xhosa. Conditions on this war-torn frontier profoundly influenced Harriet's attitude towards colonial life and the indigenous people. According to Adler she perceived the colony as a haven with 'green and undulating parks', while the land beyond the frontier

---

70. Barter, *The dorp and the veld*, p. 22.
71. Ibid., pp. 172–3. See also p. 53 and the whole of Chapter 12 in which he denies that Africans have any moral feelings or any ability to absorb Christianity. He did admit once that the ease with which Africans learnt English and Dutch attested to their equal mental capacities with Europeans; see ibid., p. 31, but generally Charles's racism was extreme. In his diary (Rickard, 'Charles Barter, Natal diary', p. 44) he referred to a colonist who was in trouble for shooting an African, and added 'I wish he had shot a thousand!'
72. R. White, *Inventing Australia: images and identity 1688–1980*, Sydney, Allen & Unwin, 1981, pp. 8–9 and 13–14.

was threatening, savage and violent.[73] Catherine also suggests this stark contrast; she refers to the Zulu a number of times as 'savages', and once contrasts the 'advancing civilization' of the Natal Colony – as represented by European hunters – with the savage population in the Zulu kingdom.[74] Catherine, when her skilled wagon-driver, whom she was slowly converting and educating, visited his homestead, employed a revealing metaphor of hell to describe his visit: it was a 'fiery trial'.[75] Catherine and Harriet shared an unquestioning belief in the beneficial effects of British imperial rule, but Catherine also stressed the benefits of Christianity and capitalism in that process of conquest and rule.[76] Africa tended to be seen as an empty landscape to be settled and exploited by the British.

Yet Catherine's account differs from Harriet Ward's, as Adler describes it, in the way in which she depicts indigenous society. Unlike the eastern Cape frontier and the Xhosa, the Natal Colony and the Zulu were not at war in the 1850s and an increasing number of colonists were annually entering the Zulu kingdom to shoot wild animals and barter for cattle and other natural products. The worst danger they faced was not from the inhabitants – who were generally hospitable and ready to act as guides and hunters – but from diseases (malaria, black-water fever and dysentery) and accidents involving guns and wild animals. Catherine's entire account clearly portrays a Zulu society that was non-aggressive towards the harbingers of empire. Although she was at pains to highlight her fears of travelling alone in the Zulu territory – these she listed as fever and 'the insolence and savage habits of the Zulus'[77] – the latter actually boiled down to one class, viz. young Zulu men who were soldiers in regimental barracks and who sometimes failed to respect Europeans' private property.[78] She does not seem to have had any fear of sexual advances from Africans, and this is consistent with many women's accounts of travel in Africa, as Callaway has observed.[79] The fact that Charles was prepared to leave Catherine with only the protection of their own African attendants shows how safe he believed she would be in the Zulu kingdom.

Harriet Ward held strongly racist fears about the Xhosa whose potential she merely assessed as a future proletariat.[80] Catherine was not free from racial

73. Adler, '"In a man's country"', p. 33.
74. See *Alone among the Zulus*, pp. 1, 2, 5 and 7.
75. Ibid., p. 9.
76. See Adler, '"In a man's country"', p. 33; and *Alone among the Zulus*, pp. 2–3 and 19.
77. *Alone among the Zulus*, p. 7.
78. See ibid., pp. 31–2 and 66–7.
79. Callaway, *Gender, culture and empire*, pp. 235–7. Callaway explores the periodic colonial masculine obsession with white women's sexuality in a situation of imperial or military domination (see pp. 237–8), but this did not pertain to the Zulu kingdom in the 1850s.
80. Adler, '"In a man's country"', p. 33.

prejudice: her use of terms such as 'savages' and 'barbaric' and her description of the physical characteristics of Africans, for instance, shows some ambiguity: certain features she approves of, but others arouse her strong aversion,[81] and there is another area where race was significant for her, which will be discussed below. But these racial prejudices were tempered by her belief that Africans were capable of being 'civilised' (a belief shared by the Colenso family) and she comments on their natural intelligence and shrewdness, particularly with regard to trade.[82] Even her bizarre belief that Africans were incapable of blushing and thereby showing shame – which is an evangelical belief – was qualified by her claim that this inability could be overcome by Christianity.[83]

Catherine depended heavily on her black attendants when she was travelling on her 'own' (without European male support), and particularly on her wagon-driver whose skills, initiative, and devoted service to her and her brother, come across clearly. She called these attendants 'my people' to distinguish them from the local Africans in the northern and remote region of the Zulu kingdom where she was feeling especially vulnerable.[84] This relationship is in contrast to her attitude towards European traders and hunters whom she avoided. (She does not explain this aversion but it may relate to gender and class distinctions.) When she returned to England, from December 1855 until early 1857, apparently for health reasons,[85] she took with her a converted African servant called variously Uluhunga or Ulurungu, who was Salome's father. Once when Catherine dined with the Moberlys in Winchester, this man had to dine with the family as the servants were apparently afraid of him; clearly neither Catherine nor the Moberlys were averse from dining with an African servant, although the novelty of the occasion remained with the author of this story well into her eighties.[86]

Catherine's travel book does, however, reveal many cultural prejudices: for instance about African 'unpunctuality', the men's supposed laziness in not building fences to keep out hippopotamus from the women's gardens (Zulu technology was inadequate to keep out these extremely powerful animals), their volubility when working together (which she found 'intolerable'), Zulu songs and singing which she found 'monotonous and uninteresting' (although she commended their rhythm), and much of their dancing she thought 'simply disgusting'.[87] These prejudices show ignorance of the

---

81. *Alone among the Zulus*, p. 20.
82. See ibid., pp. 20, 26 and 42.
83. Ibid., p. 20.
84. Ibid., p. 80.
85. Feilden, *My African home*, p. 265.
86. See Charlotte A. Moberly to George Moberly, letter dated 21 July 1931 (in private possession of M. P. Moberly), and Spencer, *British settlers in Natal*, v. 2, p. 37.
87. *Alone among the Zulus*, pp. 8, 23–4, 86 and 93.

context and nature of African society, which Adler sees as common to women travellers.[88]

Catherine was willing to use her skin colour to acquire authority and physical protection, a common strategy of many women travellers. As Birkett has said, colonialism 'stressed the importance of physical appearance, and racial characteristics were used to form an absolute distinction between the ruler and the ruled.'[89] The title of her book *Alone among the Zulus* clearly indicates how strongly she felt the 'otherness' of both her constant African attendants and the Zulu people, and it is significant that, except on one occasion when she relates an incident that occurred in Natal,[90] she never refers to her attendants by name. When seeking protection from the young men of a remote homestead after her attendants had been dispatched to find her sick brother, Catherine stressed to the homestead head the fact that she was white and a woman.[91] Later when she thought she would have to persuade Tsonga men to carry her brother and his companions to safety she remarked:

> 'My driver had already tried to do so without success; but that was not enough to deter me; he was but a black man like themselves; but a white woman, a creature such as they had never yet seen – scarcely ever heard of – surely there was yet a chance that I might prevail!'[92]

On another occasion she offered her 'powerful protection' to a Tsonga who was afraid to travel through the Zulu region on his own as he feared the 'warlike' Zulu.[93] Her consciousness of the superiority of her race and culture also enabled her to cajole – if not bully – locals into doing favours for her when she was trying to rescue Charles.[94] She was also convinced that her appearance was greatly valued by many Zulu as white women were still a rarity in the Zulu kingdom in the mid-fifties.[95]

There are some interesting ambiguities in Catherine's gender-related attitudes. Her upbringing had moulded her into a supportive, passive role,[96] but she had enjoyed a relatively privileged education and a wide social circle. She

---

88. Adler, ' "In a man's country" ', pp. 29 and 33.
89. D. Birkett, *Spinsters abroad*, (Oxford, 1989) quoted in Adler, p. 36.
90. This concerned the ability of a driver named Yakobe to remember oxen once seen, but it is not known if this was the man who accompanied her in 1855; see *Alone among the Zulus*, pp. 51–3.
91. *Alone among the Zulus*, pp. 66–7.
92. Ibid., p. 77.
93. Ibid., pp. 60–1.
94. Ibid., pp. 61–3 and 71–2.
95. Ibid., pp. 24 and 33.
96. This emerges in the entries in Charles's diary; see Rickard, 'Charles Barter, Natal diary', pp. 52, 56, 70 and 84.

clearly maintained some of her restrictive metropolitan habits in Natal, as witnessed by her dress, missionary activities and austere lifestyle.

But Natal offered her liberating opportunities. These included – at a time when middle class women in England were not permitted to travel alone and when entrepreneurial activities were seen as socially degrading – the freedom to travel unaccompanied by a male relative in the wilds of Africa, where she had many dealings with the 'savage heathens' and had to face accidents and dangers, and to engage in trade on her own (although on behalf of her brother).[97] Challenging the popular belief that women lacked a spirit of adventure, Catherine declared that she 'thoroughly enjoyed a long trek in a waggon through wild country', though she also wrote vividly of the physical discomfort and dangers.[98] She accompanied Charles twice on trips into the Zulu kingdom, in 1854 and 1855, and it was only after the latter near-disastrous journey that they gave up travel north of the Colony.

Catherine's novel *Home in South Africa* contains many of the class and gender attitudes mentioned above. The story was designed quite explicitly to encourage working class emigration to the British colonies,[99] and relates the experiences of such a couple, Molly and Robert Dadge, who emigrated to Natal, and by dint of solid, evangelical qualities and good fortune soon acquired their own property and rose in the social scale. The couple experience more equal social relations with landowners in Natal than the rigid class relations in England, shown in the opening chapter, would allow. The author comments approvingly:

'Such a case could hardly have occurred in England; but in colonial life, where people depend far more upon their neighbours, the kindly feelings between one class and another are brought out and strengthened, and I am inclined to think that a more healthy state of mind and a far greater amount of happiness result from this simple mode of life than from the more exclusive system which prevails in the mother country.'[100]

Although she approved of the relaxation of class barriers, Catherine was critical of Natal colonists, particularly for their low level of education and inability to speak Zulu. Charles, by contrast, has been criticised for being a snob; for

---

97. The only 'goods' which Catherine personally traded in were cats which were valued for their rat-catching abilities; see *Alone among the Zulus*, p. 26. This book also mentions an earlier episode (p. 17) when she was transporting a heavy load of sugar cane to Durban and she and the wagon became stuck in the middle of the Lovu River for twenty-four hours. Why was she apparently acting as a transport rider?
98. See *Alone among the Zulus*, p. 18 and pp. 11, 15–16 and 29.
99. Barter, *Home in South Africa*, pp. 155–8.
100. Ibid., pp. 125–6. See also pp. 95–6 for another example of relaxed social relations.

instance he emphasised that the ship he travelled on for his exploratory trip to Natal in 1850–1 was not an emigrant ship, the term 'emigrant', he explained, being one of reproach by then, and Sir Garnet Wolseley (a not unbiased commentator) claimed later that Barter reminded people constantly that he had been to Oxford.[101] Charles and Catherine would have belonged to that stratum regarded as acceptable to the highest level of settler society, that is the Lieutenant-Governor and the appointed Executive Councillors. They seemed to have no financial worries, though Charles never achieved high colonial office despite his efforts to manipulate the patronage system in his favour.[102] He nevertheless became a respected and quite influential figure in Natal society, particularly during the 1860s and 70s when he was one of the most prominent pro-responsible government supporters. The most he achieved was when he became M.L.C. for Pietermaritzburg County in 1865, member of the Executive Council in 1873 (but resigned the next year), J.P. for the Colony in 1874 and ended his career as resident Magistrate for the Pietermaritzburg City Division.[103]

Charles cannot be considered a member of that elite colonial social category which Ross has called – in the Cape Colony – the 'gentry', i.e. the 'relatively prosperous market-oriented farm owner-operators, almost invariably white and in general considerable employers of labour.'[104] Charles's main occupation on his 5 800 acre farm *The Start*, in the Karkloof, seems to have been horse-breeding rather than extensive cash crop production, and his lifestyle can be described as that of a leisured country gentleman and a literary dilettante.[105] We also know from his diary of 1851–2 that Charles (and occasionally Catherine) socialised not only with the leading families in the Natal Colony (such as the Shepstones and Colensos) but also with settlers from more humble origins. Charles's interest in hunting and horses would have made wider social mixing inevitable.

The gender relations in *Home in South Africa* also indicate how Catherine perceived a woman's role in colonial society. While Molly is portrayed as a

101. See *The dorp and the veld*, pp. 1 and 27; and Rickard, 'Charles Barter, Natal diary', p. 29.

102. Rickard has speculated that, despite many apparent advantages, a combination of snobbery and over-ambition, plus a stammer in his speech, might have detracted from Charles's potential as a senior colonial official. See Rickard, 'Charles Barter, Natal diary', p. 29.

103. See Spencer, *British settlers in Natal*, v. 2, pp. 39–40 and Rickard, 'Charles Barter, Natal diary', p. 30.

104. R. Ross, 'The rise of the Cape gentry', *Journal of Southern African studies*, 9 (2), 1983, quoted in G. Dominy, 'Meet the Methleys: an introduction to the Natal gentry', paper presented to the University of Natal's 75th Anniversary Conference on the history of Natal and Zululand, Durban, 2–4 July, 1985, p. 1.

105. At various times Charles edited local newspapers and on retirement wrote two popular poems. See Hattersley, '"Oxford collegian": Charles Barter', pp. 124–5.

devoted helpmeet to Robert and as a committed and practising Christian,[106] she is also full of enterprise, good sense and courage, and Catherine stresses the necessity for male settlers to be accompanied by a hard-working, stable wife.[107] Molly is aware that her husband loves, admires and respects her judgement.[108] Another female who appears briefly but in a similarly strong light in the book is the sister of the upper class man who arranges the Dadges' emigration; she also reveals enterprise and a forthright manner.[109] Catherine also believed that marital relations could be improved by colonial life; at first Robert is indifferent to his wife's inner thoughts and feelings but by the end of the book, either because of marriage or colonial life, speculates the author, he is able to express his emotions to Molly and listen sympathetically to her personal feelings.[110]

It is significant that after Salome had completed her education, Catherine returned to Natal in her early sixties, and there she died in 1895 at the age of seventy-seven. The Colony of Natal offered her self-fulfilment and possibilities for achievement which would not have been possible in the more restrictive society of Victorian Britain.

Like many women's travel books, *Alone among the Zulus* offers the reader ad hoc references to the customs and social life of the Zulu people but only brief comments on their political system. The latter reveal the stereotypical Natal colonial prejudice; the Zulu kings are simply described as tyrannical and despotic.[111] Catherine comments on the layout of homesteads (private and regimental), the Zulu language and the *ukuhlonipha* system, foodstuffs and crops, and Zulu superstition and witchcraft. Since she is supposed to have been something of a Zulu linguist, it is likely that some of this information is accurate, but much of it is indicative of nineteenth-century ignorance of the cultural context of Zulu society. She does however unconsciously reveal a number of interesting facets of the Zulu economy and social practices in the mid-1850s, which confirm much of what contemporary historical research has claimed about the Zulu kingdom in that period. These include its economic self-sufficiency (which within a year of her trip was to be destroyed by cattle sickness introduced by white cattle traders),[112] the peaceable nature of black-white relations, the generally hospitable nature of Zulu homestead heads, the shrewdness of the Zulu when bartering livestock – which indicates the

106. See Barter, *Home in South Africa*, pp. 36, 78 and 81.
107. See ibid., pp. 38, 50–5 and 142–3.
108. Ibid., p. 82.
109. See ibid., chapter 1 and pp. 12–13.
110. See ibid., pp. 81–2 and 154–5.
111. See for instance *Alone among the Zulus*, pp. 21, 40, 41 and 99.
112. This disaster features in her novel *Home in South Africa*, but relative to how it affected the Colony.

importance of stock to their social structures[113] – and the integrity of many homestead heads when handling the trade of Europeans.

Her travel book and novel also offer interesting information about trade relations between the Zulu and European hunter-traders from the Colony. Hunting and trading to obtain wild animal products and cattle hides for European markets were the main economic activities in early Natal. Catherine mentions how lucrative this trade was before the Zulu kingdom was overrun by traders,[114] and Charles was prepared to leave the business of trade to Africans and his sister so that he could engage in the more productive and 'sporting' occupation of elephant hunting. Between 1845 and 1855 the value of products of the animal trade never fell below a quarter of the Colony's exports and this remained the case until the early 1860s.[115]

There is evidence of the decline of the centralised control over trade exercised by Mpande's predecessors. While hunting and trade benefitted the fledgling Colony, hunting had a destructive effect on Zulu fauna, and the trade of Europeans has been said to have led to the underdevelopment of the Zulu political economy, particularly from the 1860s, during Mpande's reign (1840–72). This latter process related specifically to firearms and the cattle trade, the latter being Catherine's occupation while Charles hunted along the Phongolo River. Whereas Shaka and Dingane had retained control of the trade between their subjects and the Europeans, Mpande for a number of political and economic reasons gradually lost centralised control.[116] For instance, it was expected that traders would seek the Zulu king's permission to operate in the kingdom, yet there is evidence that certain hunter-traders in the 1850s neglected this courtesy,[117] and there is no evidence in Catherine's 1855 account of the Barters seeking such permission (although on the 1854 trip, Charles did visit Mpande).

Catherine's books reveal the highly unequal trade terms, and payment for hospitality or tasks, in favour of Europeans in the 1850s. The trade goods purchased by Charles for the 1855 trip included items which could not have cost

---

113. In *Home in South Africa*, Catherine also refers to the canniness of the Zulu when bartering cattle; see pp. 121–2. For more on the fundamental significance of livestock to the Zulu political economy and society, see J. Guy, *The destruction of the Zulu kingdom*, Johannesburg, Ravan, 1982, pp. 23–4 and 77; and J. Wright and C. Hamilton, 'Traditions and transformations: the Phongolo-Mzimkhulu region . . .' in Duminy and Guest, eds, *Natal and Zululand from earliest times to 1910*, pp. 65–6 and 70–2.

114. *Alone among the Zulus*, p. 18.

115. See R. B. Struthers, *Hunting journal 1852–1856 in the Zulu kingdom and the Tsonga regions*, ed. by P. L. Merrett and R. Butcher, Durban, Killie Campbell Africana Library, 1991, pp. (26)–(27).

116. For a more detailed discussion of why Mpande might have lost control over trade, see ibid., pp. (33)–(34).

117. See ibid., p. (35).

very much, viz. 'knives, beads, brass wire, and arm rings, red ferreting for head-bands, and other small articles of traffic . . .'[118] In her novel she mentions that a cotton blanket, costing 4s 6d, could buy a calf, while a blanket costing about 13s and a couple of strings of large red beads (8d each) could purchase 'very fine cattle.'[119] Nevertheless, Catherine also testifies to the fact that as time wore on, the Zulu became much more astute about the value of trade goods, a change which has been noted by other informants.[120]

It is also worth mentioning that both the travel book and her novel, *Home in South Africa*, are informative about practical details, the first regarding travel and trade, the second about daily domestic and economic life in the Natal Colony in the 1850s, all of which offer the social historian valuable information.[121] One further aspect of her writings deserves a mention, and this is their touches of humour[122] and irony. The ironical reflections in *Alone among the Zulus* are sometimes aimed at herself and on one occasion at the necessity of appearing heroic in a woman's travel account.[123] This reveals an interesting aspect of the personality of a woman who often comes across as a very austere individual.

When Catherine returned to Natal with Salome and the latter married, she built a house for the couple on her 100 acre property 'Wychwood' at Winterskloof, near Zwartkop mountain, some kilometres outside Pietermaritzburg.[124] The name of the property and its rural location are significant. In May 1883 she transferred 'Wychwood' to Salome's husband; why she did not give it to Salome is unknown, except for a claim in a local history of Winterskloof that she had approached the colonial authorities to have part of 'Wychwood' ceded to Salome, but these had been 'discreetly rejected'.[125]

Catherine died and was buried at 'Wychwood' in 1895. Charles was not there when his sister died, but she did not die alone according to a poem Charles

---

118. *Alone among the Zulus*, p. 11.
119. See Barter, *Home in South Africa*, pp. 122 and 119. These terms are confirmed in *Alone among the Zulus* on p. 54.
120. See Barter, *Home in South Africa*, pp. 120–1; and Struthers, *Hunting journal*, pp. (37)–(38).
121. In the novel she describes, for instance, what clothing to take on board ship (pp. 46–7), colonial vegetables, fruit and meat (pp. 89–90), how to wash clothes in cold water (pp. 91–2), and so on.
122. Chapter 2 of *Home in South Africa* contains some amusing letters of application from prospective working class emigrants.
123. See *Alone among the Zulus*, pp. 7, 8, 60 and 97.
124. There is still a property called 'Wychwood' at Zwartkop.
125. Christopher and Margaret Lake, *A hundred years in Winterskloof*, [Pietermaritzburg, C. Lake, 1990], see chapter 'Wychwood and the story of Salome Welayo'. I am indebted to Shelagh Spencer for this reference.

wrote, which is revealing of the nature of their relationship and which is also a typical response of the Victorian age:

> . . . I was not with thee, sister dear,
> When thy last hour was drawing near, . . .
> Yet loving hands and hearts were there,
> And tender touch and watchful care
> The pillows smooth'd, the potion gave,
> Nor wearied in the hope to save,
> But all in vain; for thou art gone, . . .
> And now in *Wychwood's* shelter'd grounds,
> Midst rural sights and rural sounds,
> Just under Zwartkop's forehead brown,
> That looms upon the distant town,
> Their slender tops above thy grave
> The cypresses incessant wave.[126]

P.L. MERRETT
PIETERMARITZBURG

---

126. Spencer, *British settlers in Natal*, v. 2, p. 38.

ALONE AMONG THE ZULUS

ALONE AMONG THE ZULUS.

BY A PLAIN WOMAN.

𝕿𝖍𝖊 𝕹𝖆𝖗𝖗𝖆𝖙𝖎𝖛𝖊 𝖔𝖋 𝖆 𝕵𝖔𝖚𝖗𝖓𝖊𝖞 𝖙𝖍𝖗𝖔𝖚𝖌𝖍 𝖙𝖍𝖊 𝖅𝖚𝖑𝖚 𝕮𝖔𝖚𝖓𝖙𝖗𝖞.

SOUTH AFRICA.

PUBLISHED UNDER THE DIRECTION OF
THE COMMITTEE OF GENERAL LITERATURE AND EDUCATION,
APPOINTED BY THE SOCIETY FOR PROMOTING
CHRISTIAN KNOWLEDGE.

LONDON:

SOCIETY FOR PROMOTING CHRISTIAN KNOWLEDGE;

SOLD AT THE DEPOSITORIES:
77, GREAT QUEEN STREET, LINCOLN'S INN FIELDS;
4, ROYAL EXCHANGE; 48, PICCADILLY;
AND BY ALL BOOKSELLERS.

CONTENTS

ALONE AMONG THE ZULUS.

—◇—

CHAPTER I.

DESCRIPTIVE AND INTRODUCTORY.

'Rude am I in my speech.' – *Othello*.

I AM a plain woman in every sense of the word: plain in person – as the looking-glass informs me; plain in dress as a matter of taste as well as of principle, for it is hardly a wise policy to draw attention by means of decoration to that which is not in itself attractive; plain in understanding, preferring simple matters to those more complicated; and plain in manner, as I have just cause to know, for the fact that I was 'brusque' was told me too often in my childhood to be ever forgotten.

I confess I have a partiality for plain speaking, which, although I have had some acquaintance with the world, has remained with me till the present day; and as the feeling has stood so much wear and tear, I believe it to be genuine.

After this preface it will be plain to the reader that my path has been a lonely one. It has been a strange one also; and the few incidents here recorded, being a narrative of some months spent among savages, being out of the common routine of ladies' travels, may, perhaps, have interest for the reader. At any rate the story is a true one. I have carefully abstained from dressing it up in company attire, on the occasion of its first appearance before the public; but have, on the contrary, endeavoured to produce it strictly in the garb of nature, like the savages whose doings it related.

It is now more than twelve years ago that I sailed from England for Natal in company with my brother, who had previously made a reconnoitring expedition thither, and had published a sketch of the colony and of colonial life under the title of the 'Dorp and the Veldt;'[1] of which, I need only say, that having read it carefully before I left England, I found it on my arrival in Natal to be so perfectly correct that I was thoroughly prepared for everything I had to encounter, and had no occasion, like many other new colonists, to be disappointed in any expectation which I had formed. I mention this, not because I believe the book in question to be the only true tale written by a traveller, – though a true tale it undoubtedly is, – but because I have found that the majority of colonists, either from having neglected to acquire proper information respecting the country of their adoption, or more often, perhaps, from a total want of imagination which prevents them from realizing what they have read, arrive with their minds in a terrible state of confusion. They expect to find the usual conveniences and accommodations of English houses and English life at home, in combination with a semi-tropical climate, and a household of savage servants; and this, notwithstanding all the anomalies and difficulties which unavoidably attend a first settlement in a young colony, however rapidly it may be advancing towards prosperity.[2]

In these days when the schoolmaster is everywhere 'abroad,' and when 'common things' are insisted on by persons of common sense as a necessary part of education, even for the lowest class of the English people, it always seems strange to me that a child should frequently be carefully instructed as to the manners and customs of countries with which Englishmen have little or nothing to do, while he is permitted to grow up in utter ignorance of places in which he himself, with thousands of his countrymen, may very possibly have to pass his life.

Why should he not be in some measure prepared for emigration? which the circumstances of his teeming country, and the instincts of its

1. Charles Barter's (1820–1904) account of his first trip to Natal (September 1850 – April 1851) was published as *The dorp and the veld; or, six months in Natal* by Orr, in London, in 1852. The Barters arrived in Natal on 18 August 1852. Further on Catherine says she wrote *Alone among the Zulus* ten years after the experiences recounted, i.e. 1865; by then she was again living in England.
2. Another factor which raised unrealistic expectations amongst settlers was the difficulty of obtaining reliable information on conditions in Natal; many over-optimistic accounts were published in Britain.

people, combine to mark out as the special destiny of the Anglo-Saxon; the possessor of the fairest and most distant portions of the earth, and the chosen instrument of peopling – oh! that we might also say of Christianizing – the various regions of the globe![3] When one re-members that we are officially solicited to judge of the teaching of the present day by *results*, one has the less scruple in observing that it is often eminently unpractical. In geography, for instance, I remember to have heard in the national school of a country village two questions asked successively, and correctly answered. 1st, 'What is Upsal famous for?' 2nd, 'Where did the great poet Byron die?' Clearly such questions as these pre-suppose a thorough acquaintance with the science in general, even among the labouring classes.

But so imperfectly is Geography really understood, that on the day of my return to England I was twice asked by individuals in highly respectable positions, 'Pray, madam, where is Natal?' and one of them added, 'Is it not in America?' and this notwithstanding the number of vessels which have plied every month for years between the ports of London and Liverpool and that of Natal, and in the face of the distressing notoriety which, as we supposed, our colony must lately have acquired through the troubles of its church.[4]

Under these circumstances my well-informed readers will perhaps excuse me if I state, for the benefit of those whom it may concern, that Natal is a British colony, on the eastern coast of South Africa, about one thousand miles to the north of the Cape; its port of D'Urban,[5] frequently called Port Natal, being in latitude about 30 S., and longitude about 30 E.

The Umzimkulu River forms the southern boundary of the colony, and the Tugela separates it from the Zulu country, the territory of King Panda,[6] on the north. The length of the coast-line, which runs in a north-easterly direction, and almost at right angles with the course of these rivers, may be about 150 miles. The country rises in successive

3. These are typical Victorian sentiments; see the Introduction pp. (27)–(28).
4. This is an oblique reference to the controversy surrounding Bishop Colenso which began shortly after his arrival in 1855 and which culminated in his deposition on a charge of heresy in 1863. This split the Church of England in South Africa and was accompanied by considerable disorder and petty squabbling.
5. The township of Durban was proclaimed in 1835 and was named after the Cape Governor Sir Benjamin D'Urban. The region had been named 'Natal' by Vasco da Gama in 1497.
6. Mpande kaSenzangakhona (*c.*1798–1872) usurped the throne from his half-brother Dingane in 1840, who had himself ousted Shaka.

terraces, terminating in the Drakenberg, or Kahlamba Mountains,[7] the back-bone of Africa, which close in the colony on the west. The area thus comprised is equal in extent to that of Scotland. The Zulu country, the scene of my adventures, is smaller than the colony of Natal which it much resembles in its principal characteristics.

The climate is of course considerably warmer, being nearer to the Equator; but there, as elsewhere, the temperature necessarily depends not so much on the positive latitude as on the altitude above the level of the sea.

The Drakenberg is frequently covered with snow during the winter, while on the sea-coast, and for many miles inland, snow or even frost is entirely unknown.

Though far south of the tropics the seasons in Natal and the Zulu country follow the tropical rule; the winter, which extends from April to the end of August, being almost uniformly dry, while the summer rains begin in September and continue with more or less intermission till March. In travelling at this season of the year, besides the usual inconveniences attending journeys in wet weather, one must take into account the swelling of the rivers, which become suddenly filled by the heavy rains in the higher districts, and rush down with great rapidity, overflowing their banks, so that it is exceedingly dangerous to cross them, the more so as but few bridges are even yet erected in the colony of Natal, and in the wild Zulu country such a thing is of course unheard of.

In deciding to accompany my brother to Natal, I was at first simply actuated by the hope of being useful to him. I never had cause to regret my determination, for one cannot be long in such a colony without perceiving that a man living alone, with none but native servants, and with no mistress to superintend them, must necessarily be, to say the least, very uncomfortable; but having made up my mind to go solely on his account, it occurred to me that I was now likely to meet with the realization of a latent hope which I had long entertained, of being at some time or other engaged in the work of missions to the heathen; they would be all around me, and in the course of my daily occupations there would surely be opportunities of trying to influence them for good.[8]

7. Catherine consistently spells Drakensberg without the 's'. The Zulu name for this range is Khahlamba.
8. The desire to serve a male relation and to convert the heathen were predominant pre-occupations for women educated in the Victorian era. See the Introduction pp.(19)–(20) and (24).

With this view I prepared myself by studying their language, as far as the books of that day rendered it possible, and with a little instruction, and a tolerably correct ear, I contrived somehow, as a child learns to speak, to make the language so far my own that I could transact any business with the natives, and could further attempt to explain to those who were willing to hear, the outline at least of the history of man, his creation, and redemption, and the practical duties incumbent on those who had the privilege of becoming acquainted with these great truths.[9]

It is not my intention in the succeeding chapters to dwell on my colonial experience, except so far as I may have cause to refer to it incidentally. I shall confine myself chiefly to the events that occurred to me and my party, during five months spent in the Zulu country – from April till August, in the year 1855.

I had passed a month there in the previous year pleasantly enough, alone with my brother, who had made a semi-trading, semi-shooting tour, and had paid a visit to King Panda. I had not myself done his majesty that honour; in fact, my crossing the border at all was an after-thought, for I was spending the time with some friends; but my brother sent the waggon back for me, and I could not refuse to join him,[10] and made a thorough holiday of the perpetual pic-nic among ever-changing scenery; after which we returned in safety to the colony of Natal.

On the present occasion my brother only wished to finish 'trading off' a few of last year's goods, which could be done chiefly by the agency of his native servants, and was himself desirous of penetrating a little farther into the interior of the country, so as to get some elephant shooting, of which he had been disappointed the year before.[11]

The elephant, it is well known, retreats from advancing civilization, and even from an increasing savage population. The hunting animal, man, is his natural foe, and he gradually withdraws from his immediate neighbourhood to inhabit the more remote districts, where, according to his limited calculation, he may hope to range the wide plain, or crash

9. These comments reveal the essentially practical and evangelical nature of Catherine's religion. Amongst her contemporaries she acquired a reputation as a Zulu linguist; see for instance E. Feilden, *My African home*, Durban, Griggs, 1973 (repr. of 1887 ed.), p. 119.
10. Presumably out of a sense of sisterly duty and as Charles was now a widower, his first wife having died in July 1853, three months after their marriage. This 1854 trip is mentioned again below; they camped in the Ngoye hills.
11. See the Introduction p. (34) regarding the role of hunting and trading in the Natal economy.

through the dense forest in undisturbed freedom. He soon finds to his cost that the spears of the savage enemies whom he has left behind, are nothing to the deadly bullets which the undaunted pertinacity of the white man brings to bear on him, even in his distant retreat; and his precious spoils are carried off in triumph to the colonial mart, which rears its splendid stores beside the very forest whence his parent herd departed, even in the memory of the intruders who now reign in their stead. His only revenge, supposing him capable of understanding it, is in the deadly climate to which he decoys his persecutors.[12] The hunters in the Zulu country are a hardy set of men; but they cannot escape the risk of the malaria fever[13] that always hovers about that region. It is felt more severely in some seasons than others; but rarely fails to number its annual victims.

I had no intention of accompanying my brother into the hunting grounds, as they can only be reached on foot;[14] but I had determined to go with him as far as possible, and then return to some place of safety – perhaps to a mission station – there to await the termination of the sport, when the waggon would bring back the ivory.

Whoever has the patience to read to the end of my story, will see how far my anticipations were realized, and my plans carried out.

After the lapse of ten years, I have been induced to occupy the first interval of rest that has been allowed me, since the events occurred, in writing the account of them, as nearly as I can, from memory; at any rate, I shall not draw upon my invention, and can safely say, that there will be nothing in this short narrative, however strange it may appear, that is not strictly true.

12. These comments and literary style bear a close resemblance to the well-known contemporary published hunting accounts, notably W. Cornwallis Harris's *Portraits of the game & wild animals of southern Africa* which was published in 1840/1. Catherine's comments here and below also indicate how scarce elephant were in the Zulu kingdom by the mid-1850s.

13. Malaria was prevalent in the St Lucia area of the Zulu kingdom and further north in Maputaland in the 1850s, but it was not known then that this disease was caused by the *Anopheles* mosquito. See the natural history index in A. Delegorgue, *Travels in southern Africa*, v. 1, Durban, Killie Campbell Africana Library, 1990, pp. 312–13.

14. This was due to the presence of tsetse fly (various species of *Glossina*) in the river valleys and low-lying areas between the Mhlathuze and Phongolo Rivers. Tsetse flies transmitted the disease of nagana from wild animals infected with a *trypanosome* (a blood parasite) to domestic animals. See A. de V. Minnaar, 'Nagana, big game drives and the Zululand game reserves (1890s–1950s)', paper presented at the Workshop on Natal in the Union period, University of Natal, Pietermaritzburg, 1988, pp. 1–2.

CHAPTER II.

'Anne! sister Anne! do you see any one coming?'
Blue Beard.

'INSPAN, and trek at once! I can wait no longer.' These words were
uttered with a heavy heart, as I stood at the door of my brother's house in
Maritzburg,[1] watching the dilatory preparations of the native servants
for my departure to the Zulu country. I must confess that on this occasion
I was beset by a vivid presentiment of danger and difficulty to be
encountered. Besides the dread of fever, which was present to my mind,
the experience of last year had made me aware of the insolence and
savage habits of the Zulus, and the necessity of protection when passing
through their country alone. My waggon-driver, on whom I could fully
rely, had not returned from his holiday, and I must therefore entrust my
precious self – for even a plain woman is precious in her own eyes – to
the care of a comparative stranger, an inexperienced driver – a little
insignificant fellow, not likely to inspire respect, and finally one who in
any emergency would simply look to me for advice if not for actual help.

As soon as our starting day was decided on, I had sent this word to our
own driver at his distant kraal on the banks of the Umvoti: 'The
Princess* says the oxen are inspanned – come.'

The messenger brought back word, 'He comes.' In fact we had no
doubt at all that he would obey the summons, as he left us with the full

---

1. This house stood on Erf 33, Greyling Street, Pietermaritzburg. Charles had named it
Sarsden Cottage.
* The word '*Inkosazana*,' which I have translated Princess, is equally applicable to the
daughter of a king, or of a petty chief. It is the form commonly used by the natives in
addressing the unmarried ladies of an English family. The corresponding name for the
master is '*Inkosi*,' or chief. — *Author's note.*

intention of returning in time, so we allowed a day or two for the unpunctual habits of a race of men who have never learned the value of time; and then my brother, who had been called by other business to D'Urban, departed on horseback, leaving me to follow in the waggon, in perfect confidence that all would be right, and that I should join him according to our agreement. He had further promised some sporting friends to meet them on a certain day at Tugela, and from thence to proceed in company with them to some hunting-grounds beyond it. Of course the guns and ammunition were with me, so that go I must. No electric wires to transmit the telegram,[2] 'I am in a fix − wait a day.' The time was come, and more than come: there was no help for it.

We packed the waggon − a white man, not a driver at all, giving his ready but clumsy assistance. It takes a driver to pack a waggon, as it takes a sailor to trim a boat. There is, properly speaking, a place for everything; but everything, on this occasion, was *not* in its place. The little driver had no wish to go with us; on the contrary, his thoughts were turned homewards, so I had to coax him at any rate to drive me down to the coast where fresh arrangements might be made; but I was terribly frightened at the danger I might incur if only from his want of skill.

Reluctantly the word was given, 'Bring up the oxen.' The reins, or thongs of undressed hide, were thrown round their horns. I kept straining my eyes towards the farthest point of the road leading to the Umvoti − the situation was critical. It put one in mind of the tales of one's youthful days, in which the heroine is always relieved from her fearful strait exactly at the right moment; but here the analogy failed. What pretensions could a plain woman have to the good fortune of a heroine of romance?

The business of inspanning the oxen was at last accomplished, the little man flourished his long whip, it only remained for me to mount and give the final order, '*Trek*;' when, lo! a tall, brown figure appears in the distance, advancing with rapid steps: 'See, boys! your eyes are sharper than mine.' 'Yes, it is he! the skilful hand, the strong arm, the firm will!' From this moment half my fears have vanished. I have no personal apprehension now.

Half an hour, and the chaotic arrangement of the baggage was reduced

2. The first telegraph line between Durban and Pietermaritzburg was only built in 1864 by a private company.

to order; each article assumed its proper place; the relieved little man was thanked for his courtesy and dismissed, and everything being now ready, I was called in to the kitchen for a moment. No sooner had I entered it than my driver brought out a tiny bag, from which he produced a card. I had written out the Lord's Prayer on it in the native language before he went away. He merely placed it in my hand, and saying, 'There is your paper,' he proceeded to repeat the whole of it. He had learned it during his visit to his heathen home.

Here was a good omen for our journey. I was indeed thankful that the impressions of good which I had endeavoured to produce had not been effaced by the fiery trial of a visit to a kraal.

We started late in the afternoon, but I knew we could now make up for lost time. We had no heavy load; the provisions and a supply of small articles for traffic with the Zulus we intended to take in at the port, where the prices are considerably lower than at Maritzburg; our blankets we had left in the Zulu country last year, in charge of a native there. I had but a scanty wardrobe, consisting chiefly, if the reader wishes to know, of skirts and jackets of various textures to correspond with the different changes of temperature, which are sure to recur in the course of every twenty-four hours; a little basket of medicines, carefully assorted by the advice of an experienced physician, in case of the dreaded fever; a few cooking utensils, a waterproof cloak and shoes, a couple of mattrasses, a tent, a Bible and Prayer-book, a volume of the 'Divina Commedia,' and two white cats, completed the list of my possessions.

Our journey to the bay was without incident, excepting that at the first resting-place one of my cats, having been freed from its imprisonment in a bag, disappeared into the darkness, and was given up for lost; but as soon as we were in motion the next mornng, she came out from beneath the 'cartel,' or swinging bed frame, and having thus proved herself trustworthy, she was never again confined, but she and her companion were allowed to forage for themselves at each halting place, and were regularly recalled to the tune of the Post-horn Galop, whenever the oxen were driven up to the waggon. In the course of the journey, after my stock had been increased to four, by a present of two fine kittens, it was a 'caution,' as the Americans say, to see them all scampering through the grass in obedience to the call, and scrambling up into the waggon to cower in their hiding-place till the noise of the inspanning subsided, when they emerged one by one, and sat quietly by my side till we stopped again.

On the morning of the third day, we drove over the high-ground between Pine Town[3] and D'Urban, which we reached at noon. I do not know a more beautiful drive than this. I believe the distance is from eighteen to twenty miles, but it takes some time to pass over it in a waggon. The road goes over Cowie's Hill,[4] which is very high, and commands an extensive prospect along the coast, looking southward over successive ridges, as far as the Umkomanzi River, and to the north disclosing a strange variety of country, the rocky broken ground that marks the neighbourhood of the Umgeni till it reaches the extensive flat near its mouth, now richly planted with sugar cane;[5] the fertile grazing lands near Verulam,[6] relieved from the usual monotonous appearance of pastures in England by high hills and deep valleys; the forest, which borders the whole coast with little interruption, and which for many miles beyond D'Urban flourishes in richest verdure; the long line of blue beyond – the great road home! The whole forms a most splendid panorama; but I think I prefer the quieter scene which presents itself farther on, as from the top of the Berea[7] one looks down over the forest at the bay itself, lying in peaceful beauty, sheltered by the frowning Bluff,[8] the tall masts of the shipping contrasting with the rounded masses of the trees that fringe the shore down to the point, from which boats are seen to put off: the town, a little way inland on the sandy flat, appearing to be enclosed in woods; the wonderful blue of sky and sea, pervaded by the brilliant sunshine, compose a magic picture, which disappears suddenly as the waggon plunges into the thick wood, brushing aside the overhanging branches of the most fragrant and beautiful flowering shrubs, and ploughs noiselessly through the heavy sand, while the

3. Named after Lieutenant-Governor Pine (1849–55) and founded in 1851 by Archibald K. Murray, Scottish settler.
4. Named after William Cowie (c.1809–1856), Scottish mechanic, farmer and elephant hunter, who came to Natal with the Voortrekkers in 1837, having married the daughter of Andries Marthinus Laas. By 1842 the Cowies were living on Laas's farm in the Pinetown district near a hill which later came to be called Cowie's Hill.
5. First introduced by settlers from the British Colony of Mauritius in 1848, sugar soon became Natal's main agricultural product.
6. Verulam was founded by the Wesleyan Christian Emigration and Colonization Society in 1850, with the settling of 400 colonists on the Mhloti River. It lay on the route to the Zulu kingdom. Catherine passed through it on pp. 12–14 below.
7. Name chosen by Captain A.F. Gardiner for his mission station established there in 1835, after the biblical 'Berea'; see Acts 27: 10–11.
8. The headland overlooking the harbour; according to W.C. Holden, *History of the colony of Natal, South Africa*, London, Heylin, 1855, p.4, it held a lighthouse and a flagstaff.

ever-increasing warmth combines with the scent-laden atmosphere to lull the traveller to repose. But for my own part, I can never sleep in a waggon while it is moving along, neither in the heat of day when so many stretch themselves on the cartel, and are tumbled about over stones and banks without being disturbed in their siesta; nor in the cool moonlight in which the native driver loves to push on, enjoying it himself, and knowing that his cattle suffer far less than by day. I cannot even lie down till the oxen have been outspanned and driven off to graze, and all fear of jolting is at an end. Neither can I employ myself as the Dutch women do, in sewing or knitting for hours as they trek onwards, nor even in reading. The motion reminds me too forcibly of that of a ship, and is apt occasionally to produce a similar effect at the outset of a journey.

On entering the town, the first person I saw was my brother, who had ridden out to meet me. He had made his purchases of knives, beads, brass wire, and arm rings, red ferreting[9] for head-bands, and other small articles of traffic, and the driver was instructed to take them up at once at the stores where they had been bought.

It only remained for me to do my part as commissariat officer, and to order a supply of flour, coffee, sugar, salt, and other necessaries sufficient to last three months at least. I had a box of tea with me: it had been sent us from England, for at that time it was almost impossible to obtain good tea in the colony.[10] I lost no time in making my arrangements, well knowing the penalty I must pay if I encamped for a night on the sand. It is full of minute insects called *ticks*,[11] which attach themselves closely to the person, especially of the newly arrived, and produce a most distressing irritation. We therefore continued our journey as soon as the oxen were rested, though we were not able to go far that night.

My brother, having seen us safely off, proceeded on horseback as before, a far more pleasant and expeditious mode of travelling. We crossed the Umgeni, the principal river in Natal, not far from its mouth, and plodded slowly on again through the sandy forest. The heat was

9. 'Ferret' is silk or cotton ribbon or tape.
10. Early experiments in growing tea on Natal's coastal lowlands had not proved viable, and apparently the imported variety was coarse.
11. There are many species of these blood-suckers in Natal; see the natural history index in Delegorgue, *Travels in southern Africa*, v. 1, pp. 326–7.

oppressive. The line of our course was now nearly at a right angle to that of our route from Maritzburg, and we must journey northwards, facing the mid-day sun, till, having reached the extreme point whither we were bound, we could turn our faces homeward, and at length rejoice to see our shadows fall before us.

Between the bay and the Tugela there are nine streams[12] to cross, and in those days there was not the shadow of a bridge. Some of them, as the Umgeni and Umvoti, are wide enough, and very often deep enough to swallow up a waggon altogether, while the smallest had capabilities in the way of mud of causing serious delay to our progress, if not actual danger.

It was early in the year, and the rains had not yet entirely ceased. In that semi-tropical region the winter, or dry season, is of course the most suitable for travelling; it was now about the beginning of April. Having crossed the Umgeni with ease, we went on courageously, and late at night, in a heavy shower, we approached the bank of the Umhloti, which flows near the flourishing settlement of Verulam. The road was so slippery that we dared not attempt the steep descent, so we tied up the oxen to the yokes, and rested for the night.

Very early the next morning, before the good folks were awake, we drove through the village, crossed the river, and outspanned about half a mile beyond it on a beautiful slope dotted with mimosa[13] thorns, and almost encircled by the winding of the stream. Here we purposed spending the day, as it was Sunday.[14] Verulam did not then boast a church or a resident clergyman; in fact it was chiefly inhabited by Wesleyans, by whom a mission to the natives had been established.

As soon as we had breakfasted I had my cushions and books brought out and laid under a spreading thorn, and chanted the Church-service by myself. Nothing is more desolate than reading it alone; but chanting is quite another thing. One hears, as it were, the echo of one's own voice, and is carried back to the choir one knows and loves best at home, and it *is* possible thus to forget that one is separated for a time from the visible communion of the faithful.

---

12. Travelling northwards the major rivers are the Mngeni, Mhloti, Thongati, Mhlali and Mvoti.
13. A common colonial misnomer for the many species of indigenous *Acacia* trees and shrubs in southern Africa. In taxonomic terms *Mimosa* is an older genus. See the natural history index in Delegorgue, *Travels in southern Africa*, v. 1, p. 313.
14. Sabbatarianism i.e. the avoidance of work and recreation on Sunday, was common among British settlers. See the Introduction p. (19).

After service I had a little talk with my driver, and read part of a chapter to him. Even at that time I was able to translate the easy parts of the Bible at sight, so as to be intelligible, though not idiomatically correct. I endeavoured to explain it as well as I could, and we had a few prayers. I did not think it wise to tax his lately-awakened attention too far.

Perceiving some huts on the opposite hill, which were not built exactly according to the usual type of native 'beehives,' I inquired who lived in them, and was told that they were 'believers.'[15] I expressed a wish to see their manner of life, and accordingly two of my men accompanied me to the huts. We had to ford the river, which was deeper than I had thought it, so that the men were obliged to hold me up, one on each side, by which means I escaped being wet above my ankles. On reaching the huts I found the usual round enclosure for cattle as in a common Kafir kraal; but the houses were fewer, and not disposed in the regular way; they were also distinguished by doorways, into which one could easily enter by just stooping a little, instead of crawling in on hands and knees.

I was informed that a baby had been born that morning, so I proceeded to visit the mother, and found a quiet, well-behaved young woman sitting on the ground, as if nothing had happened, very tidily dressed, with her head tied up in the inevitable red handkerchief – a custom, I believe, originally derived from the Malays, and imported by the Hottentots[16] from the Cape.

The other members of the family were preparing to go to meeting, the men looking in at the door to inquire after some article of clothing, while the girls from twelve years old and upwards were flourishing about outside in a sort of *demi toilette*, which I suppose they thought well to improve upon before they considered themselves presentable. They soon went off to a chapel which we saw at a short distance, and we returned to our waggon.

I do not know that these people were Christians; some of them may

15. African converts were called *kholwa*, an Nguni word for Christians. They adopted many European social, cultural and economic customs and occupations.
16. 'Hottentot' was the common colonial name for the mixed blood Khoisan peoples from the western Cape Colony, many of whom came to Natal as wagon drivers. The 'Malays' were the descendants of Muslim slaves imported from the Dutch East Indies to the Cape in the 17th and 18th centuries.

very possibly have belonged to the far more numerous class of hearers, who adopt clothing and decent manners on Sundays alone. I know, however, that there are at this moment a considerable number of baptized natives in and about Verulam, and an industrial school at work there.

After leaving Verulam, we proceeded along the Coast Road till we came to the Umhloti,[17] where we had an object to attain.

There were among our attendants three men who professed themselves able to lead the oxen; but we had tried them all in turns, and were not quite satisfied. Now, an expert leader is of extreme importance on a bad road, and our driver was very anxious to get hold of the young man who had gone with us in that capacity the year before, and had proved thoroughly efficient. Fortunately for us he was disengaged, and willing to go with us. Our retinue was now complete. We crossed the Umvoti without any trouble, and the next day joined my brother, who was awaiting our arrival at the house of a friend,[18] about twelve miles from the Border.

---

17. An error; she means the Mvoti River. The correct name appears in the next paragraph.
18. Probably Joshua Walmesley, Border Agent on the Nonoti River since 1853. See also ch. 3, n. 14.

CHAPTER III.

'When thou passest through the waters, I will be with thee.'
— *Isaiah* xliii. 2.

ON my arrival at our rendezvous, my first inquiries, after greeting our
kind friends, were directed to the state of the Tugela. I found that though
its waters had at present subsided, it was expected soon to fill again, as
there had been heavy rains in the upper country. The shooting party
which we were hastening to meet had, therefore, been broken up. We
were pressed to remain on the English side of the Border till the floods
should be over; but I was unwilling to tax the hospitality of our friends to
such an indefinite extent, and persuaded my brother to go on at once, so
that we might cross, if possible, before the river came down.

In order to be prepared for any emergency we repacked the waggon,
removing everything that might be injured by water from the bottom-
board to the cartel, which hung at least two feet above it. My own light
things were removed from the cartel, and suspended from the laths
which formed the waggon tent. There was just room for me to sit à la
Turque in front of the packages, so as to keep my feet dry, if the river
should prove to be very formidable.

We started, first through quagmires, and then through groves of
mimosa thorn till we came to the Tugela. It is not very wide at this point
in its ordinary state. I have heard it compared to the width of the Thames
at Westminster Bridge; but the sandy banks which have been scooped
away in flood time, enclose a much greater space, leaving a flat border of
sand on either side of the stream.

Just as we drew near, I remembered that there was a bag in the *voorkist*, or driving box, containing sixteen pounds of gunpowder.[1] I had it taken out and placed behind me. No sooner was this done than the waggon came down the steep bank with a jerk; the gunpowder fell forward on my shoulder, and precipitated me, head foremost, over the *voorkist*, with my hands on the footboard. Happily, the driver was seated on the box, and stopped my further fall, so that no harm was done; but I shuddered to think what might have occurred, as the wheels must almost inevitably have gone over me if I had fallen to the ground; it would have been impossible to have stopped the oxen till they reached the flat. I was much shaken and alarmed; but I had no time to think about it just then. As soon as I was sufficiently collected to look about me, I perceived that two waggons were crossing before us. This was fortunate, as we could observe and follow the course they took. The sand is continually shifting, and the road cannot be depended on. The first waggon was just coming out of the river on the opposite side; the axles were barely wet. The second waggon, as it entered the stream, dipped the footboard! It was evident the river was coming down rapidly; we plunged in, and it flowed quite through the waggon, more than halfway up the sides! The oxen were swimming, and my brother, who went forward on his horse to pioneer for the leader, had almost disappeared in a deep hole. Our Kaffir attendants, ten in number, attempted to get in at the back of the waggon; but were stopped in the most peremptory manner by the driver, who did not by any means wish to have his hind wheels weighed down into the sandy bed of the river, so they were forced to get through as they could, dancing and jumping about in the most ludicrous way, in great dread of the alligators[2] which abound in the Tugela, and indeed in most of these Natal rivers, which become wide and sandy near the mouth. We all reached the other side in safety, and most thankful I was to find myself there, for the next day the river was quite full, and one of my brother's men, who had been left to follow us, had to be ferried over; the water did not abate for the next three weeks. We could not have gone through an hour later than we did, and it was a nervous matter at the best. The duration of the suspense was short, for it does not take more than a quarter of an hour or twenty minutes to cross,unless the oxen come to a standstill, when one may be delayed for any length of time.

1. This seems an unusual quantity. The Natal government tried to control the trade in gunpowder in the Zulu kingdom through Ordinance 3 of 1848 which limited the amount that could be transported there to 10lbs per wagon or horse.
2. A common colonial misnomer for the Nile crocodile, *Crocodylus niloticus*.

I shall not easily forget what I endured in crossing the lower drift of the Illovu[3] alone early one January, when it was positively impassable every two or three days, as there happened to be a fitful variety in the amount of rain from the hills. I was taking a heavy load of sugar to the bay, when in the very middle of the river the oxen stuck fast. The men tried all kinds of expedients to make them go on, and after a long time, just as they appeared to have succeeded in inducing them to pull together, an unlucky turn wrenched out a piece of the front part of the waggon, so as to separate it from the pole, or disselboom. It was impossible to mend it on the spot, so I sent in every direction to hire a waggon to take on the load of sugar, and there I sat for four-and-twenty hours watching every bubble that rose on the surface of the stream, lest it should portend a rush of water which might carry me away, together with the property entrusted to my care. At last came a waggon from an American Mission Station,[4] and relieved me from the charge and the danger at once; but it had not been a pleasant time, though, perhaps, not altogether unprofitable.

The Tugela is almost the only river on the coast which flows into the sea without the interruption of a bar of sand at the mouth. This is a very remarkable feature. The rivers end in a kind of lake, separated from the sea by a beach of sand, through which the superfluous water oozes, so as to prevent any accumulation during the winter months; but when the heavy floods come down from the upper country in the summer, the waters gather till they overflow or burst the bar, and find their way into the sea. The southern, or right bank of these streams is uniformly high and wooded, while the opposite side is flat and bare. There is no manner of shelter near the Tugela after crossing into the Zulu country. It certainly does present a most inhospitable appearance. A tuft of high grass, or an accidental bank of the shifting sand, is a boon when it is found to windward, and rough hurdles of reed or wattle[5] are occasionally

3. The Lovu River enters the Indian Ocean a few kilometres south of present-day Amanzimtoti, south of Durban. The incident described here is tantalising – why was Catherine transporting sugar to Durban, and on whose behalf?
4. There were two stations of the American Board of Missions in this area by 1851; the Amanzimtoti (started by Dr Newton Adams in 1847) on the river of the same name, and the Mfume, south of the Lovu River.
5. According to A. Hattersley in *The British settlement of Natal*, Cambridge, University Press, 1950, p.279, the black wattle was introduced to Natal from Australia in the early 1860s. Clearly Catherine is using the term in the general sense of twigs or branches used in the construction of fences or walls.

improvised to shelter the fire during the outspan. There is a difficulty, too, in obtaining fuel. For some miles beyond the border there is a tract of uninhabited land; after a few hours trek, however, the landscape becomes pretty, dotted with thorns, and very park-like. There is an abundance of streams everywhere, so that even in winter the oxen never want water or grass.

In those days, I must confess that I thoroughly enjoyed a long trek in a waggon through a wild country. Waggons are utterly at variance with civilization; it is only in a state of nature that they are bearable.

In the course of our journey we sometimes left the beaten track, and found a road for ourselves – up a hill, and along its ridge for miles, and then headlong down into a plain, judging our route by the eye, and seldom failing to strike our point; choosing a pleasant sheltered spot to encamp for the night, letting our oxen and horses graze at will, and cutting fire-wood, or even materials for a hut, if we chose, without fear of question.

Our first stage brought us to the house of an Englishman,[6] who had been for some time settled in the Zulu country with his family. I have heard that, being pressed by demands which he found it inconvenient to satisfy, he retreated beyond the border, not to escape his creditors, but to give himself time and opportunity to settle with them all. The Zulu trade was then a very lucrative speculation, as the country had not been overrun by waggons and pedestrians, and the lung-sickness or cattle plague[7] was as yet unknown. The people gladly brought him cows and oxen in exchange for blankets and beads, and looked upon him as a benefactor, – in fact, as a kind of chief. With this position, and a re-established credit in the colony, he did not care to change his domicile, but remained for many years in the same place, living comfortably, though in a rough way, and exercising hospitality in a liberal manner. My brother went to the house; but I had no need to do so, and remained in the waggon, where I was detained a close prisoner for

6. Probably Ephraim Frederick Rathbone who came to Natal from the Mauritian Civil Service in 1848. He acquired land from Mpande on the Msunduze River, a tributary of the Matikhulu River. His home was a common stopping-place for travellers. Robert Briggs Struthers records having met Charles Barter at Rathbone's house in February 1853 (*Hunting journal 1852–1856*, Durban, Killie Campbell Africana Library, 1991, p. 28).
7. Lung sickness (bovine pleuropneumonia) was introduced to the Zulu kingdom in December 1856 when infected Natal cattle mingled with Zulu herds during the battle of Ndondakusuka. See n. 13 below.

some days by the heavy rain. Before we departed, I went down to pay my respects to the mistress, who had kindly sent me a present of vegetables. She showed me her garden, which, in addition to the usual beans and potatoes, contained some sugar-cane and arrowroot; the latter she was able to manufacture for home consumption; the patch of sugar-cane, I have no doubt, supplied the place of a confectioner's shop to her children; but the sample was sufficient to prove that first-rate sugar may be grown in the Zulu country, whenever British enterprise and capital can be carried thither with safety.[8]

A fine day saw us again in motion. The kraals of the natives were now frequently visible on the slopes above the streams. They have a picturesque effect at a distance. Their plan is uniform, consisting of two circular enclosures, one within the other. The smaller one is for the cattle; the huts are disposed in the intermediate ring, and the whole is protected by the outer fence. The hut of the principal woman is at the upper part of the kraal, directly opposite the entrance. In the Zulu country the huts are chiefly thatched with mats made of grass or rushes, while in Natal the grass is merely laid on in heaps or bundles, and tied or pegged down. The frame-work of the hut is of rods stuck into the ground in a circle, brought together at the top, and crossing each other at regular intervals, where they are tied with strips of fibre. This fabric is supported by posts driven into the ground. The floor is a work of art: it is composed of clay, stamped and beaten down, and afterwards polished by being rubbed with a large pebble. A basin with a raised border is moulded in the centre to serve as a fire-place. To the left, inside the low doorway, is a platform for the calves and sheep which are driven in at night and tied by the leg to the side of the hut. The woman's millstones are just below this platform, and here she and her children sleep. At the back of the hut are ranged the clay pots for cooking, the calabashes of sour milk,[9] and other utensils.

The finery for gala days is tied up and carefully covered to preserve it from the smoke, and is suspended from the posts or sides of the hut by strings of grass or fibre. The man's mat, his spear, shield, and other

8. This is a typical acquisitive comment by British travellers in African-occupied territory; see, for instance, Struthers, *Hunting journal*, pp. 41 and 44. Once the Zulu kingdom had been forcibly annexed to Natal in 1897, over 2 million acres were set aside for European occupation, most of which became sugar or wattle plantations.
9. Curds or thick milk, fermented in calabashes or gourds, was a staple food.

accoutrements, occupy the space to the right of the entrance. A small hurdle of wattle forms the door, and a larger one is often used as a screen to protect the fire-place from the wind.

Such are the dwellings of a race of men worthy of better things. The habits of neatness and order which they maintain, even in their present degraded state, prove that they might easily be taught to appreciate the comforts of a higher condition. The men are tall, strong, and active, and although the women are decidedly inferior, yet there are some fine specimens among them also. Their colour is, for the most part, a rich warm brown, like sepia with a considerable mixture of burnt sienna. Some few are very light. A fair woman, so to speak, is always admired. I must say that I have myself a strong prejudice in favour of the lighter shade of brown, though it is apt to pale to yellow with cold or sickness. I have seen two men who were perfectly black, but they were really frightful. The palms of the hands and the soles of the feet are invariably lighter than any other part of the body. The hair, alas! is woolly; but the flat nose, thought not uncommon, is by no means the rule – indeed, some noses remind one forcibly of the Jewish type. A great distance between the eyes appears to be a distinguishing feature, and gives an unpleasing width to the face. Its uniformity of colour is also remarkable. Neither anger nor any other emotion can call up a blush into the cheeks. This has always shocked me by reminding me of the sad text in Jeremiah: 'Nay, they were not at all ashamed; neither could they blush;' and I have indulged in a theory that the gift of shamefacedness ought to come in due time with Christianity and improved habits. I am happy to say that in the case of a child *pur sang*,[10] but born of Christian parents, who was never smeared with grease and red earth in its infancy, like the heathen children, the colour *does* mantle in the cheek, and I trust that in a future generation the reproach may be rolled away.[11]

The only kraal of importance which we passed was pointed out to me as the residence of Umbulazi,[12] one of the numerous sons of Panda. I believe the king had never formally nominated his successor, and a jealousy arose between this Umbulazi and another son named

10. Full-blooded, unmixed.
11. For a discussion of these Victorian prejudices see the Introduction pp. (28)–(29).
12. Mbuyazi kaMpande (d. 1856) was the product of Zulu levirate custom; Shaka had given one of his wives to his brother Mpande to produce children on his behalf. Mbuyazi's followers were the *Isigqoza*. See also n. 13 below.

Cetywayo,[13] who mustered a large following, and on the occasion of a hunting party attacked his brother and killed him, together with many of his adherents. The soldiers of Cetywayo tracked the remainder to their homes and murdered them. Their families escaped to the woods, where they hid themselves by day, and fled at night towards the Tugela, still dodged and pursued by their relentless enemies.

The object of Umbulazi's people was to take refuge in Natal; some of them succeeded in so doing; but the majority were killed in a terrible fight which took place at the lower drift, or ford. The river was very high at the time, and many of the poor wretches were drowned, and more thrust through with spears as they entered the water. The carnage was dreadful. Numbers of bodies were carried out to sea, and some were washed on shore at the Bay of Natal, having been brought thither by the strong current that sets down the coast.

I have lately had under my care a little girl who was discovered among a heap of the slain at the Tugela drift, and only saved from perishing by the determined humanity of an English gentleman, and the persevering kindness of his wife, who received her, sewed up the numerous spear wounds with which she was pierced, and gave the little nameless orphan a home.[14]

The battle of the Tugela occurred within two years after the time of my visit. Cetywayo is now, I believe, acknowledged as the heir apparent; he is almost as powerful as the king his father, and even more dreaded by his future subjects.

13. Cetshwayo kaMpande (c. 1826–84) had in fact been designated by Mpande as his successor when the latter had fled the Zulu kingdom and settled briefly in Natal, to escape from Dingane, late 1839–1840. But once he was king, he changed his mind and tried to argue that Mbuyazi was the real heir because he had been fathered for Shaka (see n. 12 above). But by then Cetshwayo and his supporters, the *Usuthu*, had become too powerful and the only way to resolve the crisis was by fighting. At the battle of Ndondakusuka, late 1856 – one year after the Barters' adventures (and not two years as Catherine later claims) – Mbuyazi was defeated and killed.

14. Joshua Walmesley, Zulu Border Agent on the Nonoti River, and his wife Maria, had no children, so they brought up this child as their own, calling her Nomanzi (amanzi = water; no = common prefix to women's names). According to one account she occupied an ambiguous position in the house, having been taught to cook and to play the piano. She chose to marry one of Walmesley's Zulu headmen, much to their distress. To ensure that she would be accorded great respect, Walmesley demanded a very high bride-price. See *The James Stuart archive*, v. 1, Pietermaritzburg, University of Natal Press, 1976, pp. 1–3; see also D. Morris, *The washing of the spears*, London, Cape, 1966, p. 196.

CHAPTER IV.

'Onward where the rude Carinthian boor,
Against the houseless stranger shuts the door.'

The Traveller.

ON reaching the kraal, at which we had deposited our blankets, we found
that our trust had not been misplaced. The 'umnumzana,' or master of
the kraal, had bought several head of cattle for us at tolerably reasonable
prices; we rewarded him, and left them still in his charge while we
proceeded on our journey. Turning out of the direct road we went over
some hills and descended into the rich plain of the Matikulu; the
luxuriance of the grass was unparalleled by any that I had ever seen. An
immense herd of splendid cattle was grazing there. We were told that
they were chiefly the king's oxen, belonging to one of the regimental
kraals. They had probably been taken in some raid upon the upper
country, where they are much larger than on the coast. They had many
white marks upon them; this makes them more valuable in the eyes of
the king, who uses the whitest skins to make shields for his warriors.[1]

The Zulus have a name for every mark that a cow can possibly bear;
indeed, as far as I can learn, their language is richer in this particular than
in any other. It is said that of the thousands of cattle belonging to the

1. The Zulu military system was based on age-regiments, sections of which were located at
various royal homesteads or barracks. Each regiment had a distinctive name and a herd of
cattle with similar markings, from which their distinctive shields were made. In Mpande's
time only the older men carried white shields, while the younger ones carried black
shields. See P. Colenbrander, 'The Zulu kingdom, 1828–79', in A. Duminy and B. Guest,
eds, *Natal and Zululand from earliest times to 1910*, Pietermaritzburg, University of Natal
Press, 1989, pp. 104–5; *The James Stuart archive*, v. 1, pp. 303–4 and v. 4, pp. 118, 119;
and A. T. Bryant, *Olden times in Zululand and Natal*, London, Longmans, Green, 1929,
pp. 573–4.

king, and distributed among his subjects to be tended, he knows the colour of each individual, so that if a casualty occurs, the report is at once brought to him personally, and he is able to identify the animal by the description. If the skin of the dead cow has many white marks, it is taken at once to the great kraal; but if not, it becomes the perquisite of the man who had it in charge. From the plain of the Matikulu, we soon came to the kraal of a great prince called 'Nongalazi;'[2] he was the king's uncle, and reported to be rich, so we hoped he might sell us a cow or two. We outspanned not far from his gate, but he did not appear. We sent to let him know that we were there, and after some delay he came out with a few followers, but was very short in his answers: 'He had a white man of his own, whose blankets were now heaped up in one of his huts; he could take some of those if he needed them. If my brother wanted cattle, why did he not sell his sister?' He did not, however, go so far as to offer to purchase me. It was useless to try to amuse him, he was much too gruff and cross; but we asked for some sour milk, which a man of his rank should have brought out and presented to us unsolicited. His only answer was an enquiry if we had any black head-bands, meaning dark blue ones. We had none but scarlet, and it appeared he thought those vulgar! so he informed us that he had no milk, and that he was going into his hut to sleep – it was about noon.[3] Thus ended our visit to old Nongalazi, who has since had to fly for his life, and take refuge in our country: let us hope that he was more hospitably received.

We met with no other incident worthy of notice till we reached the Umlalazi;[4] this is, to my mind, the prettiest stream in the Zulu country; it has many windings, and in some parts is full of deep holes, the abodes of the hippopotami, or sea-cows,[5] which annoy the people extremely by devouring their mealie crops. The women choose the rich ground near the river for their gardens, and of course the men are too lazy to attempt a

2. Nongalaza kaNondela of the Nyandwini offshoot of the Qwabe people was one of Mpande's principal headmen or state official. He lived at iSethebe just north of the lower drift over the Thukela. The area between the Thukela and the Mhlathuze rivers had been awarded to him by the Zulu king.
3. This surly reception from Nongalaza contrasts with the hospitality afforded Adulphe Delegorgue in 1841 by Nongalaza's wives; see Delegorgue, *Travels in southern Africa*, v. 1, pp. 167–8.
4. The Mlalazi River enters the Indian Ocean just north of present-day Mtunzini.
5. 'Seacow' is a transliteration of the Dutch *zeekoe* for the hippopotamus (*Hippopotamus amphibius*).

fence of any kind;[6] the sea-cows come out in the night, and sweep a wide path clean before them, besides trampling down the crop in every direction.

As we drew near to one of the kraals, the women met us, and besought the white man to avenge them upon the enemy, showing the desolate state of their gardens, and complaining that they should die of hunger.

We encamped on the spot, and my brother and his men watched at night for the sea-cows, but they smelt powder, and would not leave their holes.

The women were very wild and ignorant. They stared at me as I sat in the waggon, and at length asked my driver what manner of creature I was, adding a guess that I might be a young man! To this he gravely assented, and they were quite satisfied. I heard them repeating it among themselves. After enjoying the joke for some time, I descended from the waggon and had some talk with them, in the course of which I enlightened them as to the correct view of the matter; they were much pleased, for they had never seen a white woman before, and I dare say they talk of the wonder to the present day.[7]

We were now not far from the coast; the year before we stationed ourselves for a few weeks at a kraal under the Umgoi[8] mountains, nearer to the source of the Umlalazi, where I had the most delightful bathing-place, – a pool with one broad stone for its floor, and another for a dressing-room, and the whole sheltered by an over-hanging thicket, rendering it quite secluded and private. I enjoyed this luxury for a fortnight or so; but one afternoon the rain set in unexpectedly; our men were busied at once in making the hut water-tight, and in digging a trench round it to carry off the water, for it was on the slope of a hill. I was employed in stowing away the loose things in the waggon, and had no time to look about me; indeed, the mist prevented our seeing anything at a distance. The next morning, when it was somewhat clearer, I awoke to behold a considerable waterfall rushing down the rocks which formed

6. This comment is another reflection of Catherine's cultural prejudice; the Zulu had no effective means of keeping out these extremely powerful and aggressive animals. See the Introduction pp. (29)–(30).
7. See the Introduction, p. (30) for comments on Catherine's attitude to race.
8. The Ngoye hills lie between present-day Eshowe and Empangeni and about 10km west of the present University of Zululand. The highest peak in the area is 486m. A number of streams flow down to the Mlalazi River, but the source of that river lies further west near present-day Eshowe.

the back-ground of our view, and to hear that the little stream was only fordable with difficulty by two men together holding on to each other, the water being up to their necks; across this ford I had walked on stepping stones the morning before without wetting my feet.

We hovered about the Umlalazi for some little time, moving from one kraal to another. Very early one morning, while the chill mist was still on the ground, I saw one of the horses which had been blanketed and tied up to a thorn tree for the night, standing in an uncomfortable way, making a kind of arch with his back, and drooping his tail. I reported it immediately, adding that I feared he was ill; but he did not refuse his food, and nothing more was thought of it at the time. My brother rode him a part of that day, and said that he carried him as well as ever.

By-and-by we met with a party of sportsmen with whom my brother was acquainted; they were going to the elephant shooting grounds near the Pongola, a considerable distance farther in the interior. He agreed to join them, and the waggons travelled in company for some days. Having crossed the Umhlatuze we outspanned on the sand beyond it, and my brother's tent was pitched for the night in its usual position in front of the waggon, in which I always slept. In the morning, when I awoke and peeped out, no tent was to be seen. I called to the men, who speedily arose, and found that the pegs had been loosened from the sand, probably by a strong wind in the night, and that it had fallen down. On lifting up the heap of canvas from the ground they discovered their master sleeping quietly beneath its folds, totally unaware of what had happened. Fortunately for him the pole had fallen in an opposite direction to that in which he was lying.

Our next outspan was at a large kraal on the top of a hill. Our poor horse was tied up to the waggon at night, and I heard him neighing over his oats in the morning, apparently in high spirits. My brother rode him on a little way before us to explore the ground, when he suddenly stopped. His rider got off immediately, and threw the bridle to one of the boys, desiring him to lead the horse gently along while he himself joined the party in the other waggon, which was ahead of ours, to consult with them as to the remedies he should apply at the next station. Within half an hour the boy came back with the saddle and bridle; the poor animal had dropped down dead.

The other horse had been sent back at once into the colony as soon as we heard that the sickness still prevailed. In Natal it ends with the first frost in May, but we were now passing beyond the limit of frost. In fact no part of the coast is healthy for horses, though a few become seasoned to it in time.[9]

After this untoward accident we had no remarkable adventure, and proceeded at a regular pace of about four miles an hour, or twenty in a day. The country was not very interesting till we crossed a little stream, with an enormous tree growing on the bank beside the drift, and came into a very beautiful and fertile tract of small extent, where the crops of mealies and kafir corn[10] flourished in perfection.

The greatest man in this neighbourhood was Umururulu,[11] who had a kraal on a hill near the road. We outspanned in the valley, and presently down came the gentleman to ask if there were any cats in the waggon, for his kraal was overrun with mice.[12] What a lucky chance! It was my only opportunity; for being supercargo, I had taken the cats, and the cats alone, on my own private account. They were all produced at once – the two white ones, a black and white, and a grey. The two last rejoiced in the names of Euphrates and Tigris, why I have never known, except that they were once nearly meeting their death in a river. He chose the white ones, and presently his boys arrived driving a very handsome cow. She was red and white with a brindled face. Her only fault (there is always a fault in a cow if a native parts with it)[13] was that she had borne one calf and lost it. They have an idea that if this happens with the first calf, the cow is unlucky, probably bewitched, and that all her future progeny will die in the same manner.

Having great belief in care and good management with calves, and not being quite as superstitious as my friend with the long name, I closed

9. Nagana, carried by tsetse flies, and horse sickness (equine flu), were the most common diseases which afflicted horses at that time. See ch. 1, n. 14 and the natural history index in Delegorgue, *Travels in southern Africa*, v. 1, p. 316 under *paerde sickt*.

10. Common name for any of several species of the grain *sorghum*, especially *S. caffrorum*, which is cultivated to make porridge and beer. The Zulu call it *amabele*.

11. Umururulu has not been identified. Elsewhere his name is spelt Umurulrulu.

12. There about 25 genera and many species of mice and rats indigenous to southern Africa; see the natural history index in Delegorgue, *Travels in Southern Africa*, v. 1, p. 314. Bryant in *Olden times*, pp. 302–3 claims that the Zulu acquired cats from the Portuguese via the Tsonga in pre-Shakan times. H. F. Fynn gave cats to Shaka as a gift (*Diary*, Pietermaritzburg, Shuter and Shooter, 1969, p. 77) and R. B. Struthers gave a cat to a homestead head to protect his stores (*Hunting journal*, p. 37).

13. This caution in bartering livestock was due to the central importance of cattle in Zulu society. See the Introduction, p. (34), n. 113.

with him at once, and drove away my cow, which received the name of the 'Mother of Cats,' was a very good milker, and reared several beautiful calves in defiance of the prejudice against her. I fear this Umururulu was a sad scamp. I found out afterwards that he had been the chief agent in denouncing a party of American missionaries to King Panda, and had even headed the troop that was sent to murder them, and this, as far as I could ascertain, without professing open hostility.[14]

The last river that I crossed in company with my brother was the Umfolozi, which runs through a reedy *vlei*, or marsh. To avoid the unhealthy air[15] I went up the next hill, and encamped at the kraal of the most hospitable native I had yet visited. He brought out plenty of sour milk, bruised corn, and pumpkin porridge, in fact every kind of food he possessed, and instead of attempting to bargain with us beforehand, he took whatever we offered him in return. While we were there a party of Amatonga[16] arrived, carrying baskets of different kinds for sale. They were all made of *ilala*,[17] a low palm that grows plentifully on the sea-coast. Some of them were flat like bags, and beautifully woven in a pattern, the others were round open baskets of a kind common in Natal, but of very superior workmanship. They had also a number of large nuts (the produce of their own country) which are greatly in demand among the Zulus and the Natal Kafirs, who use them as snuff-boxes.[18]

One of the men had his face elaborately tattooed; I believe it is very uncommon even among that distant tribe; probably it was an old fashion, for this individual was no longer young. He was brought up to me for inspection as a curiosity. I bestowed upon him the additional ornament

14. This particular incident has not been identified but it may refer to the attack on the Inkanyezi mission (at Empangeni), under the American Board of Missions missionary, the Revd Aldin Grout, in 1842, which resulted in the expulsion of all whites south of the Thukela. This attack is commonly seen as an attempt by Mpande to secure his political position; he viewed missions as a threat to his authority.
15. Fever, i.e. usually malaria, was associated with swamps or marshy soils in the nineteenth century as these areas often harboured the *Anopholes* mosquito. See also ch. 1, n. 13.
16. Amatonga was the Zulu and colonial name for all the African groups between St Lucia and Delagoa Bay, which are more commonly known today as Tsonga, or Ronga speakers. Since Shaka's time the Zulu had controlled the trade through Delagoa Bay, using Tsonga as agents and carriers.
17. *Hyphaene natalensis*, the ilala palm, has long leaves which served a number of practical purposes.
18. The Umthongwane tree (*Pouteria natalensis*) or wild plum tree has an inedible acorn-shaped fruit which becomes red when ripe and which were made into snuff-boxes. See Struthers, *Hunting journal*, p. 51 and A.T. Bryant, *The Zulu people*, Pietermaritzburg, Shuter and Shooter, 1949, p. 408.

of a red head-band, and purchased some of the baskets for a few strings of small beads.

We now made our arrangements for a separation. My brother transferred to the waggon of his companions such of his effects as he considered indispensable, – guns, ammunition, a blanket or two, and a few clothes, besides a contribution to the provision store, not forgetting beads and other articles wherewith to purchase food from the natives. He then selected two or three men as his attendants, and bade me farewell. I prepared to retrace my steps, intending to dispose of some of the remaining goods for cattle should opportunity offer, and then to make my way to a Norwegian mission station[19] on the coast, there to await his return, or a message from him to report his own progress, or to direct my further course.

19. The Lutheran mission station at Empangeni, near the Mpangeni and Mhlathuze rivers, was established by the Revd O. C. Oftebro, under the direction of the Revd (later Bishop) H. P. Schreuder, in 1851. There is a photograph of Oftebro and his family in R. C. A. Samuelson, *Long, long ago*, Durban, Knox, 1929, between pp. 48 and 9; see also p. 3 of Samuelson, and S. O'B. Spencer, *British settlers in Natal, 1824–1857: a biographical register*, v. 2, Pietermaritzburg, University of Natal Press, 1983, p. 37.

CHAPTER V.

'Ah! now thy barbed shaft, relentless fly,
Unsheathes its terrors in the sultry air.'

ROGERS

MY party now consisted of the driver, the leader, two men, one of whom
had acted as my brother's groom ever since we arrived in the colony, a
boy of about fourteen, and a little dog called Stiggins. This dog had been
born in my kitchen, and given away while a puppy to a boy of our
acquaintance; but it had once been taken into the Zulu country, and from
that time it had acquired a taste for travelling. It lived in the same town
with us, and sometimes paid us a visit on its own account. We did not
encourage it at all; but if ever it found any appearance of preparation for
a journey, nothing would tempt it to leave the waggon, and it insisted on
going with us. It had done so the year before, and on the present
occasion; in the course of my wanderings I found it a very useful and
intelligent companion. But of this hereafter.

I think it was on the second day after leaving the Umfolozi that we
came soon after noon to a little crooked muddy drift, which we had
easily crossed on our way northwards; but it so happened that now the
oxen were tired, and there was a deep mud-hole just below the steep
bank. Our hind wheels stuck fast in it, and though the spade, and
everything else we could think of, was put into requisition, the evening
closed in before we could move an inch, and it became evident that there
we must pass the night. The men accordingly climbed the bank, and lay
down on the grass a little way off; but I had no other choice than to sleep
in the waggon. Sleep I should not say, for, to my horror, I found that I
had invaded the Court of the King of the Mosquitoes. I have often been

brought into close contact with these lively insects; but I am sure their stronghold is in this little unknown stream.

The morning relieved me of their buzzing and biting; but I had dark baize curtains to the waggon, and in the folds of these curtains they ensconced themselves to come out the following evening with fresh appetite and renewed power of worrying their victim; it took two or three days to get rid of them. They must have been deputed by their royal master to convoy the illustrious stranger on her way.

I believe to this day I am the only white woman who ever crossed that stream (I certainly could have dispensed with the honour). I have slept in river beds, and on river banks, many times before and since, for it is not at all an uncommon thing for the oxen to prolong the crossing by repeated refusals till the sun sets, and the case becomes hopeless; but never have I been so molested elsewhere.

But to return to our sheep (as the French say), or rather to our cattle: I went on leisurely, buying a cow here and there till I arrived at one of the great royal or regimental kraals, answering, I suppose, to what would be called among civilized nations the depôt of a regiment.

A circle of immense circumference like a large field is fenced in, and constitutes the kraal. Inside this fence is a row of huts for the accommodation of the soldiers and other persons attached to the place or visiting there. At the upper end, opposite to the entrance, is a very high fence, carefully constructed with wattles, and behind this are the huts of the great ladies – either old wives or mothers of the king, who are entrusted with the care of some of the royal children. *Mothers* abound in this state of society, for all the so-called wives of a man's father, or of any of his numerous uncles, are called his mothers. There is also usually one of the wives of the head officer of the regiment – I have really too much respect for the army to call such a man a colonel.

In the Zulu country every man is a soldier. The mode of raising regiments appears to be by conscription. The young men of each year are gathered together, either to form a regiment or to be added to an old one, to revive it, as they say. When a soldier has attained a certain standing he receives the royal permission to marry, and adopt the head-ring as a mark of manhood; but he is not exempted from military service till age incapacitates him. There is always a large body of men on guard at

Nodwenga,[1] the king's great kraal, where he himself resides; when he meditates a raid, he summons his troops, and arms them with spears and shields from his own armoury. One soon learns to judge from a man's age the regiment to which he belongs. They have very strange titles, and I used to amuse myself by asking the men as they approached: 'Where do you serve?' 'Are you a "Pig," or an "Euphorbia Tree?"' This regiment was called the *Isanqu*[2] – a name I do not pretend to translate. We outspanned not far from the fence, and obtained leave to put our oxen into the kraal for the night.

The young men came pouring out, asking for red head-bands. I refused to give them away, so presently they brought out bowls of sour milk and bruised corn to exchange for them. I was unwilling to disappoint them, and bought so much of the food that we did not know what to do with it; even our dog had a bowl that he could not finish.

The old ladies, hearing that a princess had arrived travelling alone, sent me a small portion of milk with a most delicious loaf of new mealies. The worst of all these dishes is that none of them can be kept till the next day; they ferment and become both distasteful and unwholesome.

When the men had obtained their head-bands, they were very curious to know what the waggon contained, especially if there were any guns. For answer, I pointed to the two empty gun cases slung on either side so as to be close by me as I lay on the cartel, and asked them if they had ever heard of a white person travelling without arms.

I must say, I was unwilling to acknowledge our unprotected state to such a wild set. These young soldiers are very insolent at times, and it was rather a questionable proceeding for a woman to go alone to a regimental kraal.

Even at a private kraal I had once seen the young men jump upon the

---

1. Nodwengu, Mpande's principal homestead, lay between the Black and White Mfolozi Rivers on the site of modern Ulundi.
2. R.C.A. Samuelson in *Long, long ago*, p. 242, claims that the 'pigs' regiment was called the Izingulube, after the name of their headquarters kraal Ezingulubeni. A 'Euphorbia tree' regiment has not been identified. Samuelson (p. 242) and A.T. Bryant's *Zulu-English dictionary*, Pietermaritzburg, Davis & Sons, 1905, claim that the isAngqu regiment was named after the Orange River, while J.W. Colenso's *Zulu-English dictionary* (4th ed., Pietermaritzburg, Shuter and Shooter, [1905]) associates it with the Vaal River. It was formed in the early 1850s and has been variously located, for instance at Okhula north of the Mhlathuze river (see *The James Stuart archive*, v.3, p.149) and at Nseleni north-east of modern Empangeni (see Samuelson, *Long, long ago*, p.248).

waggon in order to examine its contents, and though they were speedily knocked down again, I had no wish that such an attempt should be repeated.

We dismissed our visitors, and retired for the night. My men, of course, slept under the waggon; this, except in very hard weather, or for any especial reason, is the invariable rule.

In the middle of the night I heard a great noise of driving oxen, and what was worse, of angry voices. I had not slept, for I was rather nervous as to what might happen, and dreaded above all things a collision with the natives.

We had one very noisy man, who had sat up drinking with the soldiers, and I could plainly distinguish his voice among the rest. I called instantly to the driver and begged him to go and see what was the matter, and settle everything quietly, for I knew I could depend on his discretion.

After a little while he returned, saying that it was all right now; but our oxen had broken through a fence, and had been enjoying themselves in the gardens belonging to the queen.[3]

The young men declared that we should make the fence good before we left the place. The driver had wisely refrained from disputing this at the time, though he had not the slightest intention of being cheated into repairing their crazy fence. At any rate it could not be done in the dark, so the oxen having been placed somewhere in security, all subsided into quiet once more.

Early in the morning the queen sent me a yearling ox, with a message by one of their officers. They wanted salempore,[4] or blue calico, and beads for it. It was by no means a valuable animal, though it proved very useful in after years.

I made the best bargain I could for it, hoping they would sell a better one by-and-by; but they said they could afford no more.

After breakfast I went to pay them a visit. The driver escorted me to the gate of the tall fence of the *Isogoholo*,[5] or preserve of the women;

---

3. Presumably the senior of the 'old wives or mothers of the king' referred to above.
4. Salempore was a blue cotton cloth.
5. The *isiGodlo* (pl. *iziGodlo*) was the royal establishment of women who had been presented to the Zulu king as tribute, by leading subjects. They were kept in seclusion at the various royal homesteads. Apart from concubinage, and attendance on the monarch, they were mainly a means of royal patronage as the king could give them away in marriage and thereby grant status and acquire bride-wealth. It was an institutionalised form of state control over women. See J. Wright and C. Hamilton, 'Traditions and transformations: the

after he had announced me I went on by myself. The old creatures were highly flattered by my visit. They were immensely fat,[6] and tolerably well decorated with beads and brass buttons. They asked me all manner of questions, were beyond measure surprised that I could understand and answer them, and we had a long chat.

There was one article of my dress which I found always excited attention and remark. I wore a cap with a plain quilling of net round the face, and this net trimming the people took for a snake skin, and imagined of course that I must be a great doctor, as the wisdom of their own witch doctors is supposed to be derived from the snakes in which abide the spirits of their departed ancestors;[7] they habitually adorn themselves with the dried skins, winding them round their heads, necks, and body.

The ladies insisted on my waiting till they had prepared some food for me. After a long while a young girl brought in a bowl of stuff not unlike thin water gruel without salt or sugar.[8] I tasted it, and told them that I thanked them for the milk and loaf of the previous night (for which I had duly paid with a present of beads), but that in our country such food as *this* was only given to infants and sick persons. In fact, that I did not like it at all. They were not sorry, for they consumed all that I left, and I returned to the waggon to send them another little present for which they had begged.

They never made any allusion to the disturbance of the previous night. The truth was, the mealies had all been gathered long ago, and the oxen had only walked into the stubble.

We secured the services of one of the young soldiers to show us the

---

Phongolo-Mzimkhulu region . . .' in Duminy and Guest, eds, *Natal and Zululand*, p. 70. For an insider's view of domestic life in the *isigodlo* of Cetshwayo in the 1870s, see *Paulina Dlamini: servant of two kings*, compiled by H. Filter; edited and translated by S. Bourquin, Durban, Killie Campbell Africana Library, 1986.

6. One of James Stuart's informants (*The James Stuart archive*, v. 1, p. 343) claimed that the 'fatter, larger-limbed girls' who were likely to grow to a 'good size' were preferred for the *isigodlo* − see n. 5 above. Delegorgue often commented on the size of Zulu women of rank; see *Travels in southern Africa*, v. 1, pp. 92–3, 175–6, 198.

7. The Zulu practised ancestor worship. The spirits of departed family members (*idlozi*; pl. *amadlozi*) were often supposed to reside in snakes. See Bryant, *The Zulu people*, pp. 353–4, 523, 711, 731; and Samuelson, *Long, long ago*, pp. 378–9 and 390–1.

8. This may have been beer (*utshwala*) which was made from fermented grains, usually sorghum (see ch. 4, n. 10). Other travellers enjoyed this beverage; see Delegorgue, *Travels in southern Africa*, v. 1, p. 195, and Fynn, *Diary*, pp. 269–70.

way to the next regimental kraal, that of the 'Pigs,' to which we were bound. He went with us as far as was requisite, and having received the coveted douceur[9] of a head-band, returned, and left us to proceed.

We had not gone far when the hind wheel, which had been shaken in a stony drift, and was weaker in its interior than we were aware, suddenly gave way as we were going along the side of a hill. I was not at all disturbed by the accident, as happily it was the upper wheel that broke, but how to get on was the difficulty.

We examined the fracture, and made an effort, by nailing a piece of wood across it, to keep the parts together at least till we should reach the mission station, which was not far off; but three or four turns dislodged our support. It was clearly a case which could not be remedied on the spot, but required the skill of a wheelwright.

We cooked a meal, and took time to think. While we were thus engaged a waggon came in sight and outspanned within less than a quarter of a mile of us.

I conferred with my prime minister, and determined to send to the waggon, stating that a lady, Mr. —'s sister, travelling alone, had broken a wheel of her waggon, and requested the loan of one during the outspan, promising to return it immediately on her arrival at the mission station. They would have had it again by the next morning at the very latest; and as pressing on is quite foreign to the habits of Zulu traders, who make constant halts in order to see if there are cattle for sale in the neighbourhood, it would have occasioned them the smallest possible inconvenience. My messenger arrived at the waggon and preferred my request, which was interpreted to the two white men by their Hottentot driver as they lay smoking and drinking coffee. They merely laughed, and told the man to go away. Presently they inspanned again, and went on towards the military kraal we had left that morning. Before they reached the gate *two* of their wheels broke down, and they remained there, thus disabled, for three weeks or a month. So much for retributive justice. I was very thankful that their incivility had probably saved me the cost of repairing their wheel as well as my own.

Foiled in this attempt, we set our wits to work again, as our hands appeared to be useless for the present.

I remembered that I had some slight acquaintance with the missionary

9. Gratuity or bribe.

and his wife, having spent an hour with them the year before when they were returning from D'Urban in their waggon. They were resting one very wet Sunday close to the place at which I was then staying. In the afternoon, the weather having cleared up a little, I went down to see them, and found a delicate woman with a young infant. She did not dare to move from the waggon. The weather had been very wet during the three days of their journey; they had stopped for one day at a mission station, where their clothes had been washed by a Kafir girl; but they had been unable to dry them, and had perforce brought them on as they were. The mother had gone down to the bay to obtain medical assistance, and had been in extreme danger. She had not yet had time to recover her strength, and here she was in the close waggon with the steaming clothes all round her − under the mattrass − by her side − every where.

As I approached her husband was hanging out a few articles to dry, if possible, in the evening sun, but there was small hope of that. I spent a very pleasant time with them, talking over missionary work, in which, though not actually engaged, I took a very great interest, and we parted with many mutual expressions of a hope that we might meet again; but I did not then anticipate that we should come in each other's way.

To return. I now resolved to try if my friend could help me in my need, knowing that all the Norwegian missionaries are obliged to learn some' trade as a qualification for being sent abroad. What if he were a carpenter! I despatched a man at once with a note stating my case, and asking as before the loan of a wheel to enable me to come to his station. My messenger returned in due time, saying that the *umfundisi*, or teacher, was coming. He arrived the next day, and I was surprised to find that he was a stranger.[10] My friend and his wife had gone in the waggon to the bay, so his colleague had opened my note and had come prepared to do what he could for me.

The note reached him on a day appointed by the authorities in Norway to be kept annually as a solemn fast. To the best of my recollection it is the fourth Friday after Easter. I have tried in vain to discover any old church custom of which this may possibly be the state shadow.

10. The Revd Schreuder arrived in Natal in 1848 and was joined by three assistants, T. Udland, O. C. Oftebro and Larsen. If the usual incumbent at Empangeni was Oftebro (see ch. 4, n. 19), then presumably it was either Udland or Larsen whom Catherine met. There is a photograph of the Revd Udland with his wife and the Schreuders in Duminy and Guest, eds, *Natal and Zululand*, on p. 279.

The tendency of (so called) reforms in religion seems to be rather to abolish than to originate, and it strikes me that this appointment must have been a sort of compensation for something which was done away with. I should be thankful to be enlightened on this matter by any learned reader who may, in an idle hour, take up this volume. The missionary could not leave home on the fast day; but the next morning he set off with his tools.

I was truly grieved to have given him so much trouble. He was suffering severely from asthma, and had been wandering over the hills in search of me, having received very imperfect directions from my messenger, whom he had not retained as a guide.

His efforts, alas! were unavailing. There was nothing to be done but to send the wheel back into the colony to be mended.

But where could I remain while it was gone? If I could but reach the station all would be well; but with three wheels only —

We took counsel again.

I remembered to have seen, about ten miles from our present position, an empty waggon standing by the road side, with three wheels, the fourth having been damaged like our own, and taken to be mended. The waggon belonged to one of the same hunting party which my brother had joined. It was not likely to be wanted yet. Why not borrow the odd wheel corresponding with our own, and so get to the station, and return it afterwards?

Clearly this was feasible.

There remained but one difficulty: my driver must himself fetch the wheel. Under whose protection could I be safe in his absence? As far as we could see, this problem did not admit of a speedy solution, when in the midst of the dilemma there came by a walking trader, whom I knew to be a respectable person.

He had joined company with us at the beginning of our journey, during a day or two of rainy weather, and my brother had offered him the hospitality of his tent. This man, who was lodging at a kraal close by, and was well known there, offered to send two stout fellows of his to sleep under the waggon as a guard, and promised to see after me till the return of my people. This settled, they departed, going by way of the station, and cutting down a very large forked branch of a Mimosa thorn, to which they were to bind the wheel in order to drag it safely over the ground.

They returned the third day, having left notice of what they had done for the information of those whom it might concern at the kraal nearest to the empty waggon. We tried on the wheel at once: lo! it fitted exactly. Our own broken one was tied on to the forked branch, and with thanks to the friendly trader, we set forth once more, and reached the station before sun-down.

The extra wheel delayed us considerably, being dragged by two oxen, driven by our odd man. Sometimes they would turn back and perform all sorts of vagaries, at other times they would run away down hill.

The descent to the station was very steep, covered with dry grass, and exceedingly slippery. It was certainly a remarkable approach!

I held tight by the sides of the waggon tent, and trembled, fearing every moment lest the loose oxen and wheel should come in among our span, or that, at any rate, we must come to grief in some way or other. But my expectations were not realized, and we found ourselves at the station, where we drew up, by the missionary's desire, close by the side of his house.

CHAPTER VI.

Mrs. Malaprop. – 'There, Sir, an attack upon my language! What do you think of that? . . . Sure, if I reprehend anything in this world, it is the use of my oracular tongue, and a nice derangement of epitaphs.' – *The Rivals.*

My first care on arriving at the station was to despatch a messenger to my brother with the tidings of our disaster, and then to send off my driver and leader with letters to the bay, requesting that the wheel might be repaired as soon as possible. They started with six oxen and the forked branch, leaving me with the noisy groom, who prepared my breakfast and waited on me, and the herd boy, who took out the cattle every day to graze; our little dog, Stiggins, always went out with him, and used to hunt game on his own account. One day he caught a kind of hare in the long grass, and twice the boy came home with a partridge which Mr. Stiggins had killed. After a few days, thinking it desirable to gather our possessions together, I sent the man to fetch the cattle from the kraal at which we had left our blankets the year before.

He went off at day-break, and Stiggins, seeing that I was without an attendant, refused to go with the boy as usual, but kept near the waggon, followed me about wherever I went, and when I visited the missionary, accompanied me as far as the house door, lay down in the verandah till I came out, and saw me safe back to my waggon. This he repeated during the four days of the man's absence. On his return with the cattle, Stiggins went off the next morning with the herd boy, quite contented to leave some one in waiting. The missionary gave me a hearty welcome. His wife was a very good-natured person, but knew little more of English than I did of Norwegian, so that we were not likely to exchange too many ideas.

They had only one living-room, the end of it being curtained off as a sleeping apartment, so I kept to my waggon as bed-room, and, indeed, as my chief sitting-room, only going in to dine at the missionary's house, for I did not wish to tax their hospitality too far.

There were many people coming every day to sell corn, and sometimes cattle. I bought grain, chiefly mealies, for my men, and some *amabele*, or Kafir corn, for myself. When ground into meal, I found it very useful to mix with my flour, so as to economize it.

Madame, the missionary's wife, made bread of it without any mixture, raising it with sour leaven. It *will* rise, and is in this respect preferable to mealies, which do not ferment properly, so that they cannot be used to make bread without a large proportion of flour, unless one will be content with an article something between a cake and a pudding, with a very hard crust.

The Norwegian cookery is peculiar, though not to be despised. The sago soup is a remarkable dish. It is simply thin sago prepared as for a sick person, without a soupçon of meat or broth in its composition, and flavoured with sugar and spice. It is not bad in itself, but quâ soup, it is of questionable character.

The pancakes I remember were delicious; but very often we dined on porridge made of amabele meal and milk. I did not care for meat, which was rarely to be had, and my kind hosts reserved their poultry for Sundays, and other days of rejoicing, or for the exercise of hospitality, which they extended to all travellers of any respectability.

One Sunday, two traders' waggons outspanned for the day at the station, and each waggon contained the trader's wife with a child or two; they had come to make a little trip into the Zulu country by way of change, and were stowed away somewhere between the bales of blankets and the top of the waggon, which however appeared, to a casual observer, to be quite full. One comfort, or prospect of comfort there was – that a brisk sale might cause the pile to decrease, and so afford the lady more space, for with good luck, a trader's load, like that of Æsop, continually diminishes as he proceeds on his journey.

The missionary held a service in the Zulu language in the middle of the day, which was attended by some of the natives from the neighbouring kraals.

On first settling in the country, the chief pastor of the mission had requested leave from the king to teach the Truth to his subjects. He had graciously issued a mandate to all the great men in the neighbourhood of the several stations, ordering the people to assemble when called by the missionary. To-day the congregation was scanty, as all the elder or married regiments had been called up to Nodwenga, the royal residence, to move the king's kraal, *i.e.*, to build a new one not far off from the former enclosure, and consequently all the women and girls were gone to carry food to them, for beyond killing a certain number of oxen, it does not appear that his majesty thinks of providing any regular supply for his workmen.

Our traders, being quite incapable from their ignorance of the language of being themselves edified by the service, thought it desirable to command the attendance of their native servants, which they did in these words: 'Zonke umuntu oza;' which being correctly interpreted means, 'All things, person, come thou,' instead of what they meant to say, 'All people, come ye;' or, more idiomatically, 'Come ye, all people.' I mention this as a very fair specimen of the amount of knowledge of the native language usually possessed by Englishmen in South Africa.

There are many stories current which exemplify this ignorance; but I think the best I have heard is that of a colonist, who meeting with a newly arrived emigrant, offered to be his interpreter with his native workmen. They were building or fencing, and the stranger begged his friend to desire one of the men to hand him a small axe.

'With the greatest pleasure in life,' said the professor: 'Here, you! *Shaya me lo piccanini bill!*'

It is difficult to construe this sentence literally; but I *think* he meant, 'Shy me that infant billhook;' which was done immediately. The demonstrative particle *lo*, was the only word at all resembling anything in the language he intended to speak.

The Zulu language is identical with that spoken by the Amaswazi tribe above the Kahlamba,[1] and also by the Kafirs of Natal, who are chiefly refugees from the tyranny of the Zulu kings. The dialect of Kaffraria differs from it slightly; but not so completely as to hinder them from understanding each other. The Basuto Bechuana, and other tribes

---

1. The Swazi kingdom in fact lay north of the Phongolo River between the Lubombo mountains and the Drakensberg (Khahlamba) mountains. Catherine's perception was probably based on early colonial maps which depicted the Drakensberg as too far to the east.

above the mountain, speak very differently; but a close examination proves that the roots of the words, and the rules by which they are governed, are in most· cases similar. In fact, they are but different branches of the great South African language, and it is difficult to decide where the purest type is to be found.[2]

It is altogether an unwritten tongue, and therefore necessarily variable. In addition to this, there exists a peculiar custom which causes its vocabulary to increase continually. It is unlawful for a woman either to mention the names of certain male relations, or to pronounce any word resembling them, and as these names are usually taken from some object or event of every day occurrence, the ladies are obliged either to use a traditional substitute, or to invent one for the occasion.[3] These words are caught by their children, and in time become incorporated into the language. A 'woman's word' is not spoken by a man till it has thus taken rank.

The same is observed by subjects with regard to their kings. The name of the present king of the Zulus signifies a 'root,' and is also related to the word 'cave,' and the verb to 'dig, or scoop.' Not one of these is therefore spoken through his whole dominions.[4]

The tyrant Tyaka, on the death of a female relative called Umnandi, whom he was more than suspected of having murdered, issued a decree that her name should be blotted out from the language for ever. It signified 'nice,' or 'sweet' to the taste. As long as the tyrant lived every one used the word 'mtote;'[5] but when he was in his turn murdered at the instigation of his brother, Dingane, this expressive and graceful adjective resumed its place, and 'mtote,' though sometimes used, is not common at the present day.

2. According to L. Thompson, *A history of South Africa*, Sandton, Radix, 1990, p. 16, the Bantu languages are divided into two closely related languages which have a similar syntax and a common vocabulary. The Nguni – the Zulu and Xhosa (of 'Kaffraria' i.e. modern Ciskei and Transkei) – speak dialects of one language, while the Tswana (i.e. 'Bechuana') and Sotho speak dialects of the second language.

3. This describes the custom of *ukuhlonipha*, of showing respect, as it affected women; the male relatives thus addressed included sons-in-law, fathers-in-law, the latters' brothers, and brothers-in-law.

4. The *ukuhlonipha* custom also applied to the king's name, i.e. Mpande; women used the word *inkosi*. There are many references to the custom in the *The James Stuart archive*.

5. The female relative referred to was in fact Nandi, Shaka's mother. It is unlikely that she was murdered by her son; see P. Colenbrander, 'The Zulu kingdom 1828–79', in Duminy and Guest, eds, *Natal and Zululand*, p. 83. For the prohibition on speaking her name see Fynn, *Diary*, p. 136, n. 4.

I find that Professor Max Müller, in the first series of his interesting 'Lectures on the Science of Language,'[6] alludes only in the slightest and most distant way to the dialect of South Africa; but supposing his division of language into three great families to be exhaustive, I conclude that these dialects must belong to the third, or Turanian family.

The sketch of a Turkish verb, which he gives as an example, has a great resemblance to those in Boyce's Kafir grammar,[7] especially in the number of particles, positive, negative, or conditional, which are added to modify the unchanging verb.

This is a long digression, and not a very practical one. For my own part, though I can speak Zulu correctly, I would gladly see it die out in Natal, for men who have the cleverness to understand such gibberish as they often hear would as easily learn English, and so be enabled to proceed to further enlightenment.

There is at this moment among the civilised natives of Natal a great desire to obtain English teaching for their children, and I have seen several who could read well in the Bible. I have myself had pupils who could write an English dictation in words of two and three syllables with very few mistakes, and one of them writes a tolerable English letter, and is able to read what is written in answer.

The missionary was a very active man. During my stay he made an expedition into the woods to cut down timber for building. He was away three days; his wife and I spent our evenings together; but oh! the difficulty of making ourselves understood to each other. She spoke Norwegian and I answered in English as a rule; but when words and gesticulations failed we had recourse to Zulu, in which we were both at home. Strange that a barbarous African dialect should form the only available means of communication between two European women.

This has happened to me more than once in conversing with foreigners engaged in missions. The mixture of English, which on these occasions I can never forbear speaking with a foreign accent and idiom, with a word or two of German or Dutch, and the emphasis of the whole given in Zulu, would be very diverting to a bystander unaccustomed to such a style of conversation.

6. Published in London, 1861–64.
7. William Binnington Boyce, *A grammar of the Kafir language*, Graham's Town, Mission Press, 1834.

It is curious to observe how soon people fall into a way of speaking English with a foreign accent in a society of mixed races. An Irish lady who had resided for a year or two among the Dutch, said in my hearing to her little girl, 'Will you by your pappa sit?' and a little American boy made me laugh one day by saying to his mother, 'Mamma, Mr.—, there is he!' thus combining English words with Zulu construction, and enriching the whole with the genuine Yankee twang, – a three-fold union which was quite irresistible.

It is not uncommon for the uneducated persons, who form the majority of colonists, to adopt words from the native language, anglicising them after their own notion of the process. For example, Hambering from *Hamba*, to walk. Daggery, from *Daka*, mud.

When one takes into consideration that the natives on their part are adopting English and Dutch words indiscriminately, adding prefixes and terminations to them, and entirely altering them by pronouncing the letter R as L, the difficulties and complexities which sometimes arise are more easily imagined than explained. But it is time to dismiss the subject.

I had heard much in Natal of the manœuvres of the witch doctors; but had never had an opportunity of witnessing them so as to understand the principle upon which their alleged discoveries are made. I was therefore much interested in hearing that a grand consultation was to be held by appointment at the station.

It must have been, I should think, a case of great importance, for two doctors arrived together; I believe this is unusual. They took their seats on the grass, and very soon afterwards the inquirers came and sat down before them. It appeared that some relation of theirs had been suffering for a long time with pain in the chest, and they wished to know the cause of the malady and the remedy to be applied; but they remained perfectly silent.

The first doctor, who was the elder of the two, began thus:

'You are come on behalf of a man?'

'Hear!' in a subdued voice.

Dr.— 'On behalf of a woman?'

Ans.— 'Hear!'

Dr.— 'A child?'

Ans.— 'Hear!'

Dr.— 'A boy?'

Ans.— 'Hear-r-r-r!' prolonged emphatically, and very loud, the doctor having this time guessed rightly. The fact is ascertained; but he ignores it altogether, and proceeds in his guesses.

Dr.— 'No; it is a girl?'

Ans.— 'Hear!' gently.

Dr.— 'A woman?'

Ans.— 'Hear!'

Dr.— 'No; I *see*! a boy, decidedly a boy! Clap, boys, clap!'

Ans.— 'Hear-r-r-r!' with a tremendous clapping of hands from the parties interested, and the spectators who have crowded round.

Dr.— 'Has he a pain in his head?'

Ans.— 'Hear!'

Dr.— 'In his stomach?'

Ans.— 'Hear!'

Dr.— 'In his chest?'

Ans.— 'Hear-r-r-r!'

Dr.— 'In his foot?'

Ans.— 'Hear!'

Dr.— 'In his leg?'

Ans.— 'Hear!'

Dr.— 'No! I *see* it; in his chest!'

Ans.— 'Hear-r-r-r!'

And so on as to the kind of pain, its duration, the symptoms attending it, &c. &c., with which, after much guessing, the friends unwittingly make him acquainted.

As soon as all the necessary information had been thus elicited, the first doctor relapsed into silence, and the second, after going aside for a few minutes, stretching out his hands, and pretending to inquire of the spirits in a way that reminded me very forcibly of Balaam[8] and his incantations, returned and said 'that he had seen, had seen a young man – a boy – with a pain, a pain in his chest,' &c., &.; in fact, he recapitulated the whole case, and put it into the form of a narrative or statement. When it was concluded he paused to hear the renewed acclamations and clapping of hands, and to watch the admiring expression on the faces of his dupes.

The first act of the comedy was now played. The condition of the

8. See Numbers 22–24.

patient was ascertained. The more difficult part remained – to discover the cause of the illness and its proper remedy.

Let not the reader suppose that any knowledge of the laws of Nature or of Hygiene was required to settle this question. The disease must be produced by supernatural causes alone.

It is probable that the doctor may have obtained from his assistants a sketch of the family circumstances of the patient, for he proceeded to elicit by guesses in the same way, that 'long ago' an old woman had been defrauded of a cow, or that some other fatal mistake had been made in connection with a cow and an old woman, the result of which *naturally* was that some spirit (either of the forefathers generally, or of the old woman in particular) could not be appeased but by the death of the unfortunate boy who had in some way inherited a share in the transaction, or by the sacrifice of an ox. This is the inevitable conclusion – an ox must be sacrificed.

The elder doctor then took up his parable and summed up for his brother, as his brother had done for him; but with more and more vehement gesticulations; and the party, after due applauding and clapping of hands, retired to sacrifice the ox, to pour its gall upon the hut containing the sick person and others connected with the affair, to have a grand praising of the spirits, to put aside some of the best meat for *their consumption* during the night, and finally to devour the whole of the sacrifice with a good appetite no doubt, and with much noise and sour beer; but with what result to the patient does not appear.

It is the easiest thing in the world to puzzle one of these doctors. You have only to guard against raising your voice in approbation when he happens to guess rightly, and he is foiled at once.

I myself confused a doctress of great reputation by simply standing behind her, and telling her that I was the servant of One far greater than her spirits, and that I knew she could not go on with her (so-called) enchantments if I did not choose.

The people have all a great horror of being 'overlooked.' I suppose it arises chiefly from the dread of being stabbed, which is incident to such a perfect form of paternal government as now prevails in the Zulu country, and indeed has existed from time immemorial throughout the various tribes of South Africa.

One of the witch doctors, whom I saw at the station, was in the habit of coming every Sunday to be instructed, or rather to sit under instruction, for I cannot think he was anxious to carry away much of the teaching. However, they are uniformly the shrewdest men of their tribe.

I met with a remarkable man of this kind while I was residing at a church mission station on the coast of Natal. He attended with much interest to the teaching of the clergyman, who had frequent opportunities of private communication with him. During a long illness which preceded his death, though he was not so far converted as to desire baptism, or even to adopt civilised habits, he formally delivered his only son, in the presence of the elders of his family, who were witch doctors like himself, into the care of the clergyman, requesting him to bring the child up in the ways of the white men, till he should arrive at years of discretion. The boy, who manifests an unusual degree of intelligence, was baptized at the station by the name of Gabriel, and received the first rudiments of education there. He has lately been removed to the Metropolitan's College[9] for native boys at Cape Town, where I understand he is doing well.

9. Zonnebloem College for Coloured and African students was established by Bishop Robert Gray, first bishop of Cape Town.

CHAPTER VII.

'Here rests his head upon the lap of earth,
A youth to fortune, and to fame unknown.'
Gray's Elegy.

THE hospitality of the missionaries was unbounded. In fact, it was done as a matter of duty, and partly of necessity.

During my stay, there arrived a sick man who had had the Zulu fever many successive years. He was now recovering from a slight attack of the complaint, and brought with him a young man, much more seriously ill than himself, whom he had found far in the interior, walking, because his horse had died, and reduced to great weakness by the fever and the dysentery which usually accompanies it. He had taken pity on the poor youth, and had not only given him a place in his cart, but also carried his ivory, of which there was a large quantity.

Mr.— was very glad to deposit his charge in one of the mission buildings, where we soon provided him with a bed by filling a large bag with dried grass. He looked quite comfortable there on the day after his arrival, when I went with the missionary's wife to take him some gruel. It struck me that he was weak, and I suggested that he needed some stimulant.

The missionary was afraid to give it; he argued that there was still a little fever, and that other symptoms existed, which seemed to him to forbid the use of spirits, or of anything of a heating nature. He did, however, give him a little anisette, or some cordial of the kind, with which he was provided in case of need. The poor fellow was pleased with it, and said he thought he should sleep.

The missionary looked in upon him the last thing at night; but in the grey dawn of the next morning, he was summoned in great alarm by the two Kafir servants of the sufferer who had been left to watch by him. He suffered now no longer – his sleep had proved to be the sleep of death.

He was a fine young man, and though his constitution had undoubtedly been injured by the exposure and hard living to which Zulu hunters must be subject, yet with my present experience of Zulu fever, or malaria fever generally, and the effects which follow it in a semi-tropical climate, I think it is just possible that we might have saved that life by the careful administration of brandy, combined with such light food as we had by us.

I mention this with one object only, that of dispelling the prejudice against fortifying the sick, which is so very common among their friends.

In a wild country – indeed, in almost any new colony – medical attendance is obtained with difficulty, owing to the scattered state of the population, so that even if a doctor is called in once he cannot visit the patient frequently; professional nurses are few, and the sick person is necessarily cared for by those of his own household. Having a general idea that he has been suffering from fever, they imagine that he must be kept low, forgetting that the moment the fever is gone the system needs restoring, or must sink under the ravages committed by the disease. I have heard that men who go into unhealthy countries for the purpose of sport, devote themselves most tenderly to any one of their number who is taken ill; but as soon as the fever is over, they have less scruple in leaving him for several hours, and the patient often sinks away when they think him safe and in a fair way to recover.

I have myself shared the fear of being too liberal with wine, quinine, nourishment, &c., &c.; but I am sure that as long as one does not place these remedies in the patient's own hands, but administers them carefully, watching him at the same time, one is not likely to go far wrong.

In the present case, I might myself have supplied what I now believe to have been needful, had I been fully aware of it at the time; but experience comes slowly and painfully, and I have no reason to think that others who were present had ever been led to take the same view of the case as myself.

The good missionary, having done all that lay within the limits of his knowledge and power, proceeded to order a grave to be dug for the poor young man, on a grassy slope below the station, by the side of some others who had, like him, returned from their dangerous expeditions to die there.

The body, clothed and bound up in a blanket, was carried to the spot, and then the missionary, after chanting a few sentences in Norwegian, in a peculiarly solemn and church-like tone, addressed the natives who were present in their own language, endeavouring to improve the mournful occasion to the benefit of his wild congregation. He added a short extempore prayer for them, after which he directed that the grave should be made up to a neat mound, and with his own hands laid the sods on the top of it in the form of a cross.

The whole ceremony was very simple and touching. We left the poor young man in his nameless grave, hallowed only by that cross of sods, and by that old Norse chant and prayer. I believe he was scarcely more than twenty years of age. I was glad to have been present at this service; we were only four Christians there – the missionary and his wife, myself, and the kind friend who had brought the young man to the station, and who had barely strength to follow him to the grave. He suffered from the exertion at the time; but I have understood that he afterwards recovered, and braved the dangerous climate again.

Of all the trials incidental to a residence in a hot climate, I think there is none more severe than the awful suddenness which attends the removal of the departed.

The progress of disease is, for the most part, rapid; (in my own case, it so happens that I have never seen death in any way that touched me nearly which was not actually sudden;) the difficulty of arranging with any amount of decency for burial, together with the imperative necessity for haste, entirely deprives the survivors of that calm waiting time in which they are secluded from the world, and learn by degrees to bear the dread separation from the beloved one, or at least to be reconciled to the void which the sudden removal of one of its members, however insignificant, must leave in a household.

In some cases, within my own experience, the day of death – and that a sudden death – has been necessarily the day of burial. The hurried preparations have had to be made as decently as the time allowed, and a night of watching has been followed by a day of hard and distressing work, till the grave has closed in the evening over the object of our care.

During the twelve years I spent in Natal, I have been obliged with my own hands to measure and mark out no less than three graves, and to stand by and superintend their completion.

I have seen a father dig the grave of his first-born child, make its little coffin, and lower it into the earth; and a mother, with whom I was well acquainted, was herself obliged to prepare the body of her only child for its last resting-place.

On two occasions, as in the instance before us, I have heard a layman read prayers at a funeral; once I had to do it myself.

It is well if the frequent recurrence of these scenes does not render people callous to them, and altogether indifferent as to the manner in which this sacred duty is performed. I believe the American Society was the first to establish a mission station in the Zulu country; but their teacher was forced to fly in the night to save his life, which was threatened by the king.[1]

The Norwegian mission has been at work there for some years. It has only one regularly ordained pastor,[2] who lives in the higher and more inland part of the country. He is a clever man of great force of character, and speaks Zulu with so perfect an accent and idiom that it is impossible to detect the foreigner by the ear alone. He was settled at one time in Natal, and finding it necessary to purchase an estate on behalf of the mission society, he took the oaths of a British subject in order to do so. Since his removal to the Zulu country he has had the opportunity of redeeming his pledge by giving timely notice to the Natal government of the hostile intentions of their savage neighbours.

The other Norwegians attached to the mission, of whom there were

1. The first Zulu mission was actually that of the Revd Francis Owen of the (Anglican) Church Missionary Society, but this only lasted for about five months and closed when Dingane clashed with the Voortrekkers in early 1838. Catherine is referring to the second Zulu mission, set up by the American Board of Commissioners for Foreign Missions in 1840; it was broken up in 1842 by Mpande; see ch.4, n.14.
2. Probably the Revd H.P. Schreuder (1817–82) who was finally given authority by Mpande in 1851 to open mission stations in the Zulu kingdom. His first station was at Empangeni (1851) near the coast (see ch.4, n.19), but subsequent stations were established in the higher regions of the Zulu kingdom such as at Entumeni (also 1851), Mahlabathini (1860), and Nhlazatshe (1862). There is a photograph of Schreuder in Samuelson, *Long, long ago*, between pp.48 and 9.

several in the days of my acquaintance with them, occupied the position of catechists. There have since been some German teachers[3] among the Zulus, and we have now a Church Mission in the upper and more healthy part of the country, headed by a clergyman who understands the native language and character, and who was at one time intimately connected in his work in Natal with the late lamented Bishop Mackenzie.[4]

He has obtained from the king permission to make three settlements at the distance of about a day's ride from each other, and is seeking for a brother priest to help him in his lonely work. It is a free and fair field of labour. Would to God that his hands might be strengthened by a band of devoted men like himself!

I omitted to mention that, as soon as we arrived at the kraal where our blankets had been deposited, my brother had despatched two parties of Kafirs in different directions with parcels of goods to trade. Having disposed of all that they carried, they made their way to me at the mission station, and I had a day's work in hearing their report of each head of cattle they had bought, and the amount given for it in cotton, blankets, salempore, or beads.

They did not bring me the cattle; but I took a list of them from their description. They had left them with their respective owners to be collected in passing through the district again on their return.

A native never forgets a cow which he has once seen; though a white man may very often do so. A curious story occurs to me as an exemplification of this peculiarity.

During our residence in Maritzburg my brother's span of oxen strayed to a distance. We sent two men to look for them, and after spending many days in the search, they found them all except one – a yellow ox called Suirland. The driver continued to explore the country; I believe he even had recourse to a witch doctor for information; but without success. At last, after wasting two months in this way, he arrived one afternoon in

3. After the Zulu civil war of 1856 (see ch. 3, n. 13) Mpande asked Schreuder (see n. 2 above) to send more missionaries, but as the Norwegian Lutherans lacked personnel, Schreuder asked German Lutherans from the Hermannsberg Mission Society to assist.
4. Probably the Revd Robert Robertson who established the (Anglican) KwaMagwaza mission station in 1860. Previously he had managed the Mlazi mission station in Natal where Archdeacon Charles Mackenzie had assisted. The latter was later consecrated Bishop of the Central African Mission at Magomero in the Shire highlands (present day Malawi) where he died of fever in 1862. See Samuelson, *Long, long ago*, pp. 5–6 and photographs and biographical sketches between pp. 48 and 9.

high glee, driving the ox before him. It had been found on a Dutchman's farm some miles from town, and its improved condition testified to the quality of its keep. In fact, the ox (which had been reduced by a long journey just before he was lost) was now so changed in appearance that his owner did not know him. Within ten minutes afterwards came the son of the boer, riding at headlong speed, vociferating in Dutch, and accusing our driver of having stolen his ox. The driver, who had learned his trade among the Dutch, and knew their ways, answered him in his own language that it was his bass' ox.

All our Kafirs confirmed his assertion; but of course a Kafir's word goes for nothing, and the Dutchman only added an adjective to the epithet of thief, which he had repeatedly bestowed on him before.

Our English labourer was called; he had been about cattle from his youth. He could by no means swear to the ox. Neither could our next neighbour, a good-natured Irishman, though he was particularly inclined to be friendly. My brother was still unwilling to give up the animal, trusting his driver's word; but corroboration was wanting.

The boer began to triumph. He talked faster. 'The ox was a young ox,' he said; 'he had bought it himself from Over-berg only last season; it had never been inspanned: he would fetch a friend at once who should confirm his word.' He rode off accordingly.

The moment he was gone, Yakobe said, 'Now we shall catch him! He says the ox has never been inspanned! Bring the yokes! make haste!'

The whole span was grazing in the wide street before the house door; the road not having then been cleared.

I never saw the Kafirs work with such a thorough good will.

The yokes, which had been put aside in the stable, were brought out in a twinkling, and fastened to the *trek-tow*, that was secured to the disselboom or pole, and the oxen were inspanned at once. When it came to Suirland's turn, the driver merely said, 'Suirland, yoke,' and he put his neck under the yoke immediately, to the great satisfaction of the bystanders. Yakobe, who was a very good whip, then started his oxen, and drove them round and round in front of the house. He kept up this novel style of pirouette till the young boer returned with (as it happened) a sensible German friend.

'Here is your young ox that never was inspanned,' cried the driver; 'now whose is it?'

The boer still attempted to talk, but the tide had quite turned against him, and his German friend, after a word or two with my brother, advised him to go away quietly, and consider himself mistaken, to say the least of it.

The business of reckoning with my men and sending them off again occupied me for nearly a whole day.

I had to select such goods as appeared by their report to be best suited to the demand in the different directions in which I sent them. Of course, this depends on circumstances. In one district, perhaps, the people have supplied themselves lately with blankets, and are not prepared to purchase new ones.

On the other hand, a wedding, or some great feast or dance is approaching and the women-kind are clamouring for blue stuff to make cloaks. They buy enough for two breadths, and sew them very artistically together, the seam goes down the middle of the back, the garment being thrown over the shoulders, and the two upper corners brought together and tied round the neck. This is *de rigueur* at dances, and on all occasions of ceremony. Beads are *ad libitum* according to the means and extravagance of the wearer.

Large beads, or eggs, as they call them, are much valued; but there is a fashion in these things, as well as in the last new bonnet at Longchamps.

A man buys a very good blanket; he observes that it is bordered with one black stripe; he represents this to all his neighbours, and for the time all blankets are at a discount which have not the exact stripe.

Another year a red blanket is introduced, and coveted by every one. Certain kinds of beads also have their run, and are no longer in vogue. There are a few sorts, as the small opaque red and white beads,[5] which are always in demand. The traders are at their wits' end to imagine something new, which, after all, may not exactly coincide with the savage taste. In the year that I visited the Zulu country a wonderful hit had been made by a lucky trader, who, having brought some red comforters with him, and finding that scarlet decorations for the head were in unusual request, unravelled the comforters, and sold the worsted

5. Even beads were affected by fashions in taste; see D. W. Hedges, 'Trade and politics in southern Mozambique and Zululand in the eighteenth and early nineteenth centuries', Ph.D., School of Oriental and African Studies, University of London, 1978, pp. 141–2, and Bryant, *The Zulu people*, p. 158. The latter quotes Bishop Colenso who noted that in the early 1850s, the most popular beads were a small, deep-red bead (*umgazi* for 'blood') and a small, white bead (*ithambo* for 'bone').

in lengths. It received a name, and became from that time a favourite article of traffic, so that it was regularly asked for at every kraal. These small things do not of course form the staple of the trade, though it is quite necessary to be provided with them.

A cow is generally supposed to represent either a woollen blanket, two cotton ones, or a certain quantity of blue salempore for the women's cloaks. The beads are in addition to the price, as a few odd shillings might be added to a pound; and the demand for them varies with the owner's estimate of the animal's value, and with his own assurance. I have known a man ask for a blanket and ten strings of large beads as the price of an old cow, and, after driving it away in high dudgeon, eventually take a blanket for it without beads at all. In fact, they will ask the most absurd prices, and calculate on being beaten down. A native who is about to sell a cow will say, 'I shall ask such and such a price, and, if that is refused, I will go down to so and so, but not lower.'

I never saw anything to equal it except among the French market-women, who invariably ask for their cabbages, and cauliflowers, and their *bouquets de soupe*, about four times as much as they intend to accept.

It is quite necessary, on one's first visit to a French market, to be chaperoned by an experienced housekeeper, who initiates one into these mysteries, so that on the next market-day one comes prepared with a coolness equal to their own.

Having already gone through this part of my commercial education among a highly civilised people, I was not so much surprised to find the same phenomenon exhibited by a race of savages.

CHAPTER VIII.

'Haste for thy life – post haste!'

AFTER remaining about three weeks at the station I was much pleased to see my men return from D'Urban with the wheel, or, more properly, with a new one, for the repairs had been so extensive that I do not think much of the old wheel was left. The waggon had originally been built in the Old Colony (as the Cape settlement is usually designated in Natal), and had been sent by sea from Algoa Bay.[1] It was remarkably strong and very safe, especially on sloping roads along the sides of hills, the wheels being made to *flare* outwards, so as to give greater width.

The driver of the waggon we had robbed followed closely upon my own people. He also had returned from D'Urban with his mended wheel. We gave up the one which had helped us so opportunely, and once more stood firm upon our own basis.

After a day's rest (for he was very foot-sore and weary) my driver began to take thought for his gear. He found that several of the yokeskeys were missing or broken, and accordingly he conferred with the missionary, who gave him permission, as lord of the manor, to cut down a thorn-tree to make some new ones.

It was St. Barnabas Day,[2] and there was no lack of its traditionary brightness, though it fell in the middle of winter. I varied my usual routine by dining with my first friends, the missionary and his wife whom I had met in Natal.[3] They had returned home during my stay, and

1. Modern Port Elizabeth.
2. 11th June.
3. See ch. 4, n. 19.

showed me every kindness in their power. They dined soon after noon, and the meal being over, and every one busy again, I went back to my waggon, and sat there inspecting the progress of the yokeskeys. They are simply straight pieces of wood, which slip into the yokes, and come down on each side of the ox's head, having notches in them to which the throat-strap is attached.

The thorn-tree had been sawn into pieces of the required length, one man was splitting them up to make yokeskeys, while another rudely shaped them with an axe; the driver himself was to finish them off. I was talking to the men, and expressing my wish that we could hear some news of their master, when we saw a file of natives approach carrying ivory.

I sent for them, and at once began to question them.

'Whence do you come?'

'From the Pongola.'

'Whose ivory is that?'

They gave the Kafir surname bestowed by his attendants on a well-known hunter.

'Have you seen or heard anything of the party of — ?' naming the owner of the borrowed wheel, who happened to have received no fancy appellation from the Kafirs.

'Of — ? Yes; they are all dead!'

This sounded very terrible; but the Zulus make but a slight difference in their idiom between sickness and death; so it might equally mean they are all sick. However, I must own that the first impression on my mind was that they were all dead. My agitation enabled me, as any strong excitement is apt to do, to make my inquiries more rapidly and precisely.

'Listen now,' said I, 'answer me truly; are any really dead?'

'Yes, princess.'

'Let me hear,' and I began to count off the individuals of the party on my fingers; 'there were six of them. Is the head of the party well?'

'He has been ill, but can walk again.'

'How is the tall man?'

'He can walk a little.'

'There are two boys. What of them?'

'They are still alive, but very sick.'

'There were two more men – do you know anything of them?'

'One man is dead, and one is sick.'

'Can you describe the dead man, or the living one?'

'No, princess; we only heard of them by report. We know for certain that one white man is dead. There is another besides those you have counted – he is ill also.'

It appeared that another man, whom I had met on the first day after I had left my brother, had followed on the track of the party, and come up with them. I had not been aware of this, and it puzzled me. I counted them off again. Putting this additional man out of the question, the one who had died was either the driver of the waggon or my brother. It was utterly impossible to guess which of the two might be the survivor!

Was he yet alive? At the best he was ill, and would need nursing – Had I not left home in expectation of this very need?

I had no doubt as to my course of action. I thanked the ivory-carriers for their information, and they passed on.

'Now,' exclaimed my driver and I simultaneously, 'we must trek down there, and see for ourselves.'

I went to my friend the missionary with whom I had dined, and stated the case to him, asking his advice. He saw no alternative for me than to go at once, if I had the courage to do so. He came out and spoke to my driver about some arrangements that were to be made, and lent him a draw-knife to expedite the completion of the yokeskeys.

As soon as they were done I had some of the heavy goods removed from the waggon, and placed them under the missionary's charge. I retained only such things as I knew would be required, and preparations were made for an early start on the morrow. We departed accordingly with many kind farewells and good wishes from our hosts, and we endeavoured to make all possible haste, knowing that delay might be a matter of life or death. In fact, the driver said, 'We must not spare the oxen; it will be nothing if they suffer so that we come in time to save the master.'

We had only travelled for a few hours when we met one of my brother's men carrying his gun, which he delivered to me with a note. I tore it open. It was written in pencil, dated from the Pongola, and stated in a few words that he had been seriously ill with fever, but was now better, though still unable to walk; that he must be carried for a long distance to meet the waggon, which he begged me to send at once, or, if the wheel were not yet returned, to borrow another waggon without a moment's delay.

So far we were right in having started, and there was still hope of being of use to him.

The boy told us that all the men had been ill, and that the white driver had died. In fact, he gave us substantially the same account which we had received the day before from the ivory-carriers. He had himself been attacked with the fever, and had spent a long time on the road, being so weak that he walked with difficulty. He rejoiced in the name of Buffalo! I desired him to get into the waggon, and we travelled for three days, early and late, as fast as the oxen could go.

One evening it poured with rain, but we went on nevertheless; we could not afford to lose time. I knew too well the importance of attending to a recovering patient, lest the slight remnant of strength left by the exhausting fever should die away for want of due support.

On the third evening we arrived at a kraal close to the Umfolozi, and drew up there to pass the night, intending to cross the river early in the morning.

When I awoke, the first person who presented himself to my view was a tall boy who had gone with my brother. He had left him only three days before, and though very weak from the fever, and grown taller and thinner than ever, had not spared himself in his master's time of need. He carried a note addressed to me, written on a scrap of paper with a pencil as before, but in a very shaky hand, merely saying that if help did not come in a few days it would be too late − he must die of starvation.

We took the tall boy into the waggon, inspanned at once, and crossed the river. There was nothing else to be done but to press on. We were now travelling through an entirely new country, but I cannot say it ever occurred to me to notice what it was like.

In the middle of the second day's trek from the Umfolozi, as we approached two kraals standing at a little distance from each other, we saw a waggon drawing near from the opposite direction. As it seemed to be going towards the kraal on the right hand, we turned to the left, for I always made a point of avoiding other travellers when we outspanned to rest.

Before long we perceived that it was the waggon belonging to the shooting party which my brother had joined, and that two of them were in it. As soon as they discovered who I was, one of them came across to tell me what had happened.

They had had bad luck during the earlier part of their expedition, and had not seen an elephant at all. At last their scouts reported that a herd was in the neighbourhood, and they resolved to make an encampment there. They took some pains to select an elevated spot, in order to be free from the effects of unwholesome air, and found a beautiful station on the top of a breezy hill, which they thought could not be otherwise than safe and healthy. But, alas! the wind came over a pestilential marsh, and brought with it the noxious exhalations from its steaming waters. Before any one of the party could have a shot at the long-sought elephants, fifteen of their number, some black and some white, were stretched on the ground with fever.

The gentlemen, having strong constitutions, and having primed themselves beforehand with quinine, held out longest against the disease. The white driver, who was an Africander, and had led a very rough life, gave way at once, and died after a few days.

The provisions being likely to run short, the two whom I had now met, as soon as they were sufficiently recovered to walk, set off to make their way towards one of their waggons, which was coming to meet them with fresh stores. They left behind them two sick men who could just crawl about on their hands and knees, a boy one degree stronger, but still very weak, and another boy, a servant, who was in extreme danger.

The care of this helpless party was confided to one of the sick men, who was calculated from his character and position to take the lead among them, but who, in point of strength, was perhaps the least able of any, excepting only the dying boy.

In reading accounts of expeditions into countries which are dangerous, either from the hostility of the natives, or from the climate itself, one observes that in case of the party being compelled to retreat, the order of march is uniformly to place the weakest members in front, the strongest bringing up the rear, and taking such risk as may occur. This – whether in the prairies of America, the wilds of tropical Africa, or, indeed, in any region beyond the limits of civilisation – is well known to be the constant rule, a point of strict honour. I was, therefore, the more surprised to find the case as it stood.

I inquired where the sick men were to be found. They were at the kraal of a native called Umgiba, or Umjiba;[4] and the route by which I could approach it was thus described to me:–

4. This individual has not been identified.

'It is possible to go round by St. Lucia Bay in a waggon, – at least, a Dutchman did so two or three years ago, – but it is a long way round, and will take you some time. The other road by which we have walked is more direct; but if you go that way you must take care of your oxen, as there are no habitations for many miles, so that they must sleep in the *veldt*, where the lions abound. There is one river only in the way which will give you any trouble; there is at present no ford by which a waggon can cross it, but you will easily dig one out. The plain, too, is full of mimosa thorn, the branches of which will need to be lopped away as you go, to allow space for a waggon to pass. Beyond the river and the plain you will come to a wood; a day's journey through that wood will bring you to the kraal. If you find it impossible to drive through it, the sick men must be carried, or helped to walk, till they reach the waggon.'

This was encouraging, upon the whole, for a woman alone with three native men and two sick boys as her retinue!

Such expeditions as these, if made at all (for no oxen had ever been known to go where it was suggested that I should take mine), are only attempted by hardy adventurers travelling with guides or pioneers, who literally make a road before them as they go.

Sometimes, if the traveller is a person in authority, he harnesses men in front of the oxen to assist in pulling, or to encourage them to proceed. It is also frequently requisite, if the road slopes much, to place a number of men on the higher side with thongs attached to the waggon, so that, by pulling with all their might, they may keep it from turning over. This sort of thing is common in a route such as was now indicated to me, where wheels are unknown.

Being thus more than satisfied as to the kind of road I must travel, I proceeded to ask about supplies, knowing from my brother himself that he was dying of hunger, and did not expect his strength to last till succour came.

'Were there sheep or goats to be had?'

'No, not one all along the road. I must obtain them at these kraals if possible.' Finally I asked for, and received a very small quantity of tea, and we parted.

A council of war again.

We resolved, at any rate, to obtain and prepare some food at once, and to send it to my brother, and then to press on with all speed as before.

Now it chanced that at the mission station there was a man from the

Amatonga country, towards which we were journeying. It is beyond the northern limit of the Zulu dominion. Panda's subjects being a warlike tribe, in the habit of making inroads on their neighbours, the Amatonga, who are a very peaceful set of people, are terribly afraid of them, and an *Itonga*,[5] alone, does not dare to pass through their country. I had, therefore, undertaken to extend to this fellow my powerful protection, so as to enable him to return to his home, on condition of his directing us in the right way.

I proposed to send on the groom with the guide to carry the provisions. Now to procure them!

Seeing many goats grazing close by, I sent for the head of the kraal and told him I wanted to buy one.

'A goat! There is no such thing here.'

'No such thing? There is a whole flock of them.'

'They are not mine.'

'Not yours? Are you not master here?'

'Why, certainly, I am master; but they belong to the young men, the soldiers of the king; and they are away at the great kraal.'

This he said very pompously, intending to impress me. There was a report just then that the king contemplated a raid in some direction, probably across the Tugela,[6] and some of the regiments had been mustered accordingly.

'It is unfortunate that the owners of the flock should be absent, because I have a blanket – a real *woollen* blanket, not a cotton one – which is *desirous of buying a goat* (so runs the idiom), and it is not every day you find *woollen blankets* wanting goats! Why it is the price of a cow!'

This, and a good deal more, passed between me and the master of the kraal; but I spoke little myself, and chiefly through my driver, wishing to assert as much dignity as possible. In vain – the man decidedly refused to trade with me.

I was determined to have one, cost what it might, as my brother's life

5. For Amatonga see ch. 4, n. 16. An *itonga* refers to the singular.
6. According to recent research, this is highly unlikely, as Mpande appears to have respected the agreed borders with the Colony of Natal, especially after the British demonstrated their power at the battle of Boomplaats, against a Boer force, in August 1848. See J. Wright and R. Edgecombe, 'Mpande kaSenzangakhona *c*.1798–1872' in C. Saunders, ed., *Black leaders in southern African history*, London, Heinemann, 1979, p. 52.

appeared to depend upon this last chance of procuring animal food; so I sat close under the waggon, screening myself behind the driver, and hiding my face with my hands from the public gaze.

The great man, after thus declaring his final resolve, withdrew into his harem, and began to tell his assembled women about 'the wonderful white Princess who could speak.'

(To speak a strange language is not supposed to merit the name of speech, and is distinguished by a different word.)

Immediately the whole kraal turned out to see the curiosity. They began by saluting me, 'Princess.'

I was silent, and did not lift up my face.

'Princess!' (Aside) – 'They said she could speak.'

I desired my driver to say that my brother was dying of hunger, and that I could not speak to people who refused to sell me food for him.

He repeated my words.

Great dissatisfaction, and more asides; then attempts to approach.

These I resisted, having at least the right to the ground under my own waggon.

After more consultation between themselves they retired, and I occupied myself in making two loaves with some flour I had in the waggon. I raised them with carbonate of soda, and put them into the baking pot, or camp kettle, with fire under and over them, after the manner of colonists and Devonshire cottagers. I then left the men to attend to the fire, and returned to my hiding-place.

Presently the women and girls came out again from the kraal, bringing a bowl of pumpkin porridge, and another of sour milk, with its accompanying basket of bruised corn. They set all this down before me, and told me, 'that it was a present! They did not sell their food to me.'

'What is this? (I exclaimed, very angrily) take it away; I do not want such stuff! My brother is dying for want of meat, and I will not touch the food of those who have plenty of meat, and yet refuse to sell it to me, when I offer them such a price, too – a *blanket* for a goat!'

Now, nothing in the world disappoints these people (and, indeed, all who are in earnest in their hospitality) so much as refusing to partake of that which they offer.

Besides, I must have given a present in return for it, so that hope was disappointed also.

They saw I was really vexed, and that the matter was serious. They said nothing, but left the food there, and retired within the enclosure.

After a long time, a man arrived with one of the goats, a large, scraggy grey animal, with but little flesh on its bones – evidently an antiquated member of the flock.

The tide had clearly turned, so we resolved to pursue our advantage.

'That old thing for this splendid blanket! Shall I sleep in the cold to buy a bag of bones? When I have killed it, I shall still want meat. No, no! my blanket is not for such an *old woman* as that! When I have bought the best goat in your flock you will still be my debtors. Do you think I ask a favour of you? It is I who confer a benefit upon you. Take away the old thing immediately! And here, some of you, fold up that blanket, and put it into the waggon again; I will have no dealings with such cheats!'

This was completely successful. The rejected one was driven away, and a young man presently appeared dragging a nice young black she-goat by the horns; it was in thorough condition and fit to kill; but they still made a feeble protest that it belonged to a man who was absent, and – 'they had doubts!' I told them the owner would praise them indeed for their wonderful purchase, and desired my men to kill the animal at once. This was soon done. The inside was allotted to my servants, and half of the meat was put by to send to my brother; the driver insisting on my keeping the other half for myself, as it was not probable I should taste any other meat for some time.

As soon as my loaves were baked, I took them out, allowed them a little time to cool, and put them into a bag.

We then rubbed a little dry salt into the meat, and I told the groom to go off at once to my brother, repeating to him all the directions I had received as to the route, and sending the guide with him.

I need not say, that as soon as the goat was irrevocably mine, I exhibited myself most graciously to the assembled sight-seers, answered all their questions, accepted their present, and bestowed one in return.

All our party therefore had eaten and were satisfied; but the groom and the guide were not at all pleased with the order to start by themselves.

They represented to me that 'the sun had set' (it was about an hour after noon). I informed them, that if that were the case, it behoved them to make haste, and reach a sleeping-place, for that I should take care they did not sleep there; in fact, I prepared to start without delay.

We drove on through an interminable plain, the waggon shaking terribly from the unevenness of the ground, which was boggy at intervals.

At length, after a long, weary drive, the sky became overcast, and it was evident that rain was impending, therefore we outspanned in haste in the middle of the veldt, and went supperless to bed.

CHAPTER IX.

TEU'S KRAAL – LEFT ALONE – PIG DRIVING – A LETTER.

'Awkward animal to drive is a pig – very!'
Hampshire Clown.

THE rain which had brought us to a stand-still the night before, continued without intermission till the next morning; but there was no time to be lost, so we pursued our way over the tedious plain.

On this day I first came in sight of the gnu (*Catoblepas gnu.*)[1] It is a horned animal of about the same size as an ox, with a mane and tail something like those of a horse. The herd was not far off, and the creatures stood and stared at us for some time, and then suddenly started off at an awkward gallop.

This was almost the only incident of the long dreary day; but towards five o'clock in the afternoon we came to a prettier part of the country, and at length we entered a small, wooded *kloof*, or hollow of rough precipitous ground, with a stream at the bottom of it. This we crossed by as steep and unpleasant a drift as I had ever gone through, and climbed up a corresponding ascent to the kraal of Teu.[2] It was very large, and unusually well fenced, having above the gateway a little hut, in which a boy slept at night, and kept up a large fire to scare away the lions which abound in these parts.

My driver brought up his waggon as close as he possibly could to the fence, outspanned his oxen, and had them driven away; he then put everything in the strictest possible order, more so than usual for a night's outspan. When this was done he came to me, and said, 'We must go.'

---

1. There are two species of wildebeest (gnu) common to South Africa: the blue or brindled (*Connochaetes taurinus*), and the black (*Connochaetes gnou*).
2. Teu has not been identified.

'Whither?' I inquired.

'To our master, to see what has become of him.'

'This very evening,' said I, almost involuntarily.

'Princess, there is no time to lose.'

I felt that he was right, for I had perceived from the manner of the messenger whom I had sent with the provisions, that we could not place much confidence in him; but I had not yet realized the present necessity.

'But what am I to do?' I asked.

'We will speak to the master of the kraal, and ask him to take charge of you.'

'Very well,' I replied; 'pray go and call him; we will do it as formally as we can.'

The great man was then summoned to appear before me.

He came with some attendants, saluted me with the words, 'I see you, princess,' the Zulu equivalent for good morning. He then sat down, expecting me to speak.

I returned his greeting in the most gracious form with which I was acquainted: 'And I see you, father.' I then continued: 'I have sent for you to speak on business. You know the party of So-and-so who passed this way two moons since to go to the Pongola?'

'Yes, I know them; they left their waggon here and their oxen. The waggon is now gone away with two of them.'

'Do you remember one of the white men in particular?' (Here I described my brother.)

'Yes, he did remember him. Moreover, he had left an article in his charge.' (I think it was a pillow.)

'Well, you must know that I am the sister of that white man, and I am come here because I have heard that he is dying.'

(Fortunately for me, tidings of the disaster that had befallen the party had reached Teu's.)

'Now, as we only know all this by report, I must send my men on to Umgiba's kraal to find out the truth, and I myself wish to remain here. Do you consent?'

'Certainly, princess.'

'Well; but you see I am a woman, alone. My two strong men must go, and I shall have only two sick boys with me. They have recovered from the fever; but they are weak — they can do no work. Now white women

are afraid when there is no one to take care of them, so I wish to ask you if you will take care of me while I remain alone, as if I were your own daughter? I shall of course live in my waggon, and I shall be willing to buy any food you can sell me. I shall be happy to see you, and talk with you and your women; but you must give your young men orders not to come spying about my waggon, or poking among my things, because I do not like young men to bother me.'

'It is well, princess; I will tell them.'

'Besides this, I want you to take charge of my oxen, and let them go in and out with your own, and sleep in your kraal. In fact, you must be answerable for them; and then, my brother, if he comes back, or I myself, if he should not come, will give you a reward.'

Teu assented to all that I required of him, and I dismissed him with thanks for his courtesy.

I had no reason to be afraid of being left alone here, because the place was well known, and much frequented by white men, who were in the habit of leaving their waggons and oxen here while they journeyed on foot into the interior, as this was the last kraal of any size or importance.

Beyond it there was a large tract of uninhabited country, full of game of various kinds. The rhinoceros and elephant are not uncommon, the quagga[3] (*hippotigris quacha*) and the gnu, to which I have already alluded, together with bucks, or antelopes of various kinds.

The lions are in great force, and range the whole district in search of prey, especially during the dark nights of the waning moon.

At that time they will approach the dwellings of the natives, and even leap the kraal fence, where a white or light coloured ox is sure to be the victim, being more easily distinguishable in the darkness.

Our ox, Suirland, which had so narrowly escaped from the boer, was the only one of our span for whose safety I was apprehensive, the rest being chiefly dark or spotted. I determined to keep my eye on the oxen, in order to detect any injury or appearance of sickness, and for the rest to trust to the vigilance of my new protector.

---

3. Probably Burchell's zebra (*Equus burchelli*), the Dutch word for which was kwagga (hence the anglicised name of quagga), rather than the real quagga (*Equus quagga*) which was similar, but rapidly extinguished in southern Africa. Grout claimed that quagga did not belong to the fauna of Natal; see B. Ellis, 'Game conservation in Zululand (1824–1947)', B.A. Honours essay, University of Natal, Pietermaritzburg, 1975, p. 12, n. 67.

Matters being thus satisfactorily arranged, my two men set off, intending to sleep that night at a small kraal which was the very last in the district, and then to walk all day, and reach Umgiba's by the next evening, there being no other resting-place in the way.

I retired to my waggon, which was so near the fence that I could hear every word that passed within the enclosure. My two boys were accommodated in one of the houses, and Stiggins, as in duty bound, mounted into the waggon, crept inside the *voorklap*, or canvas curtain, which hangs down in front, and slept at my feet, so as to be ready to defend me.

Our oxen were driven in at sunset with those belonging to Teu, and delivered into the charge of a young man named *Umlungu*, who slept in the upper story over the gateway, and kept up the watch-fire. His name meant 'white man,' and though I was fully aware of it, yet it often startled me to hear (as it seemed) a white man suddenly addressed; and occasionally, when the call surprised me in my sleep, I went through all manner of speculations as to who the newly-arrived stranger might prove to be, before I fully awoke to the reality of the situation, and was able to remember that the 'white man' in question was of the same colour as his neighbours.

On the morning after my arrival, one of the women brought me a basket of underground beans[4] ready cooked. I bought them for a few white beads, and found them delicious, with the addition of a little pepper and salt, and amazingly satisfying. This underground bean, as its name implies, is one of the leguminous plants. Its leaves grow on long footstalks, and are divided into five segments, and its flowers are small and yellow. The seed pod is kidney shaped, and of a hard texture, containing often but one seed, or at the most two, which are closely packed together; they are of a dark purple, or red colour, with a little white speck in the centre of one side; in fact, they have all the essential characteristics of a bean. The manner of cultivating it is, to put in the seeds about two feet apart, and to earth up the plant gradually as it grows and spreads; the flower is allowed to peep above ground, but as soon as the fructification is completed, the plant is almost entirely concealed,

---

4. Probably the African ground bean, *Voandzeia subterranea*, which is widely cultivated in the tropics, although Catherine's description only partly tallies with that in F. W. Fox and M. E. Norwood Young, *Food from the veld: edible wild plants of southern Africa botanically identified and described*, Johannesburg, Delta, 1982, pp. 223–4.

and the seed ripens beneath the soil. It grows well in the thorn country of Natal, which is richer and more fertile than the other kinds of land. Its produce is abundant, but as the crop takes six months in coming to perfection, it would not, I suppose, be a profitable one. I have often planted these beans, and found them a very acceptable addition to my stock of vegetables.

Another kind of food, with which I first became acquainted at Teu's, was the ground or oil nut.[5] Its growth is very similar to that of the underground bean; but though I have since cultivated it myself, I regret that I am not able to speak positively as to the character of the flower. The seeds are enclosed in a case, and have a taste resembling that of nuts. They are sometimes eaten raw; but are much improved by being warmed on a shovel or iron plate, and are rendered more wholesome by the process. I believe they are extensively cultivated in Natal for the sake of the oil they contain; and they must be a profitable crop, as the proprietors of oil mills gladly purchase them from the producer. They are only suited to the lower part of the country, near the sea, as they ripen in the winter, and are too delicate to bear the frost.

I had one basket of a bitter kind of potato, shaped like a hand with fingers.[6] I bought it from curiosity, but took good care never to be deluded into repeating the experiment. My boys thought them excellent. They are not common in Natal, having been replaced by a long kidney potato, not originally indigenous, but which now goes by the name of the 'Kafir potato.'[7] No food in common use among the natives can be compared with the sweet potato (*Convolvulus batata*).[8] It grows like a weed from slips, and forms tubers of great size and delicious taste. It has two great advantages to a careless cultivator: it spreads and propagates

5. The ground nut or monkey nut, *Arachis hypogaea*. Fox and Norwood Young, *Food from the veld*, p. 201.
6. There are many varieties of bitter tubers in southern Africa; this particular one has not been identified.
7. According to Fox and Norwood Young, *Food from the veld*, (pp. 245–6) the 'kaffir' potato or elongated native potato is *Plectranthus esculentus* (also *Coleus esculentus*), and is called *ibonda* by the Zulu. Bryant, *The Zulu people*, (p. 273) identifies the *Coleus esculentus* as the *izambane* in Zulu, which he describes as a small tuber with an agreeable taste.
8. The sweet potato (*Ipomoea batatus Lam.*) was also used medicinally and for making starch and alcohol. The leaf was also eaten. J.M. Watt and M.G. Breyer-Brandwijk, *The medicinal and poisonous plants of southern and eastern Africa*, 2nd ed., Edinburgh, Livingstone, 1962, pp. 68 and 307.

itself when once planted, and does not degenerate so speedily as most plants are apt to do under negligent treatment. It is indeed a most valuable article of consumption, and is much used by all the settlers in the lower districts of Natal, as well as by the natives themselves.

The women, finding that I readily bought the produce of their gardens, often came to see me, and I had a good deal of conversation with them. One day, as I was entertaining a circle of them, a young man ventured to approach. He was warned off instantly by the women, and reminded 'that the Ummunzana[9] would be very angry.'

I saw clearly from this that my request had been strictly attended to, and was much reassured by the incident.

I acted on my resolution to inspect the oxen every day. They found plenty of good grass, and began to recover from the effects of their hurried journey. One of them, I was sorry to find, was rather lame. I had his hoof examined, and discovered that it was attacked with a disease called hoof-sickness, of which I had often heard, though I had never met with it hitherto. I had some salt rubbed into the sore part. I believe it is the remedy generally adopted; but the poor beast did not recover for some little time, and I feared that we should not be able to use it in case of a summons to trek. My driver and leader left me on a Friday afternoon.

In the course of the next day a native man walked up to my waggon, and, after the usual greeting, informed me that his name was Pig; that he was returning from Umgiba's kraal, where my brother was lying, to his home on the banks of the Umfolozi; that my brother had told him to desire me to send him some medicine, and to give the man a reward for conveying the message. He added that he had met my two servants on the road. He did not bring a note, probably because my brother was too weak to write.

I thought I could send nothing better than quinine and brandy, and asked him if he could take it back for me?

'Not he; he was going straight home.'

I therefore inquired where Teu was; and, being informed that he was behind the kraal very busily engaged, I went to him, and found him seated on the ground with a number of other men, occupied, if I remember rightly, in cutting out a shield from a cow-skin, and of course plenty of talk was going on, and calabashes of sour beer passing round. I

---

9. The correct spelling is *umnumzana*, i.e. the homestead head.

told him I had come to ask him for a messenger to carry some medicine to my brother who had sent for it. 'Could he lend me a man?'

'Oh, no! The young men were all gone to the royal kraal, having been summoned by the king. Those who then sat with him were on the point of departure. There was no one at home but Umlungu, and he was employed in herding *my* oxen.'

In fact no help could be obtained. I saw that my friend Pig must go, or no one; so I returned to him.

'Now, Pig, you will go back to Umgiba's, and carry the medicine to my brother to save his life!'

'Impossible, princess! I must go straight home; even now I have been expected for a month.'

'That is well! If they have already waited so long, they can wait a day or two longer; and you know it would not delay you many days. You see these beautiful arm-rings. (The Pig's eyes here opened wider.) Well! if you take this medicine to my brother, and bring me back a paper to assure me that you have delivered it, they shall be yours, besides a reward for the message you have brought to-day; but, if you refuse to go, I shall give you nothing, for you have had no trouble with that message; this kraal is in your way, and words are not heavy – they do not weigh a man down.'

The Pig here became extremely obstinate and disagreeable. 'To have nothing for his trouble! It was too bad – he was being cheated, &c., &c.'

'Softly, Pig,' said I, 'you are altogether mistaken. Here are three articles which you will receive for your trouble when you return.'

'But I am not going, indeed.'

'Not going . . . Where did you hear that falsehood? for a falsehood it is! Now listen; I do not ask you to go in the least – I have no right to order you, and it is not worth my while to coax you to do what I wish; for I look in your face – you – the pig – and I *see*, quite positively – for I am a great doctor, and am never mistaken – that you have a good heart, and that you *will* and *must* go; you cannot help it! Therefore, here is the parcel and a note; take care of them both. And look! I have put the arm-rings aside, for they are yours, and the other article for delivering the note to me to-day. Good-bye – stay, here is some food for you before you start. I do not like my people to go away hungry. Now, that is all – go!'

And it was all. He kept on saying, 'Wow! Princess! Wow!' But he went, and that was all I wanted. I was quite tired when the struggle of wills was over.

I spent the Sunday at Teu's quietly enough. On the Monday morning I went down to the river to wash some clothes, as I had had no opportunity of doing so during our forced march, since we left the Mission Station. I found a pleasant sheltered place, where I was able to enjoy a bathe myself, as well as to complete my 'lessive,'[10] and I had spread all my things out on the grass to dry, when a hunting party came by with spears and dogs. They did not appear to have killed any game, but it was evident to me, that despite the king's summons, there was still a number of idle young men left in the neighbourhood, and that Teu, being a person in authority, might have found me a messenger had he been so disposed.

I soon gathered up my clothes and went home to my waggon, taking a bucket of water with me, for I did not like to trouble my poor weak boys more than I could help. I had to dose them with quinine every day, to enable them to perform a few indispensable services for me on the spot; but the river was some distance from the kraal.

On reaching the waggon, I was extremely surprised to find a letter on the *voorkist*, directed to my brother. I enquired who had brought it, and was told that a white man had passed by on foot who had made enquiries for me; but on hearing that I was at the river, he had said it was of no consequence, and had merely left the letter. The people could not tell me whence he came, nor whither he was going.[11]

I was not ambitious of making the acquaintance of any of the traders, so I was very glad that the bearer of the letter had come and gone without meeting me – I little knew the debt of gratitude I was to owe to that man.

I remember nothing more that occurred at Teu's excepting the arrival of a waggon belonging to a well-known trader. It was sent to await the ivory which his hunters were expected to bring from the interior. It is customary for the traders to hire natives, in Natal, who are good marksmen, and to send them with a common gun, and a certain amount of powder and lead, reckoning with them on their return, according to the number and weight of the tusks they bring with them. These men

10. A rare word for washing (i.e. clothes-washing); also the word for a lye (or alkaline solution) made from wood-ashes or soap-suds which is used for washing.
11. This was Alexander Forbes; see ch. 10, n. 3.

sometimes obtain the assistance of the Amatonga to carry the ivory, and on this occasion the waggon had been sent in order to hasten the arrival of the valuable property at the bay.

The trader was not there himself, and on talking with the native driver, I found that he had lately been ill with Zulu fever, and had quite recovered.

I remembered, on my first journey towards the Umfolozi, to have met a waggon in which a man was lying unconscious on a heap of ivory, and to have heard the Kafirs say that they were taking him home to die; and on comparing notes with this driver, it turned out that he was the identical man, well, and strong, and able to drive again as before.

I noted the fact for my encouragement, for though naturally of a sanguine temperament, I was so depressed at this juncture, that I thankfully seized on any trifle which might augur a happy termination to my anxiety.

CHAPTER X.

'A friend at need
Doth gould exceed.'
Posy of a Ring.

ON Tuesday morning, soon after I had finished my coffee, I saw, to my great delight, my two men approaching. The driver brought a few lines from my brother, scrawled with a trembling hand – the last letter he ever expected to write.

He was so weak that there was no hope of his recovery unless he could be moved to a more invigorating air, and it did not appear possible to obtain bearers. To walk, even a step or two, was quite beyond his power; he could barely crawl across the hut, and his last words to the driver had been, 'Open the door that I may see the sun once more before I die.'

Nevertheless the driver, who was a sensible man, and had seen much of illness, had not yet given up hope, because, as he assured me, his eye was still bright, and his voice strong.

On this tiny ray of hope I had to live so far as to be able to act.

I proceeded to make further inquiries, and heard that on the Friday evening, after leaving me, my two men had reached the kraal on the outskirts of the wilderness, where they found the messenger, whom I had sent with the meat, kept by the rain, forsooth! The guide had refused to go on, and the groom was naturally afraid. It requires some resolution to set forth alone in an unknown country, and the dread of fever is very strong with all these people, so he had been contented to follow the old rule, 'Every man for himself.' There was no alternative but to let him sleep there; but he was routed out in good time the next morning, and the four arrived at Umgiba's together, having met Mr. Pig on the way.

The loaves which I had sent had become dry and musty before the men reached the kraal; but they had made some broth of the goat's flesh, which had been very grateful to the invalids. They were three in number – my brother, a young man who had joined the party after I left them, and a boy of about sixteen. He was domiciled with my brother, and was so far recovered that he had crawled out when they were pressed by hunger, and shot a wild pigeon or two from the trees close by.

The young man lay prostrate in another hut unable to get about at all, while they could scarcely manage to go to him. The servant boy left in their charge had died two days after his master's departure, and they had had the greatest difficulty in burying him out of their sight. Of course in such a work no persuasions could induce their heathen hosts to lend them the slightest assistance.

The natives have an intense horror of touching a dead body, especially that of a stranger. The poor fellow whom I had sent with tidings of the broken wheel, had lain down by the roadside and died as he was following his master back from the Pongola. It was grievous to be unable to wait and render him some assistance; but the invalids were being carried, and they dared not stop their bearers lest they should set them down and run away, so they were forced to let him lie there, and press on for their very lives!

It was a terrible story. Umgiba at first objected to receive them; but, as long as he saw a prospect of gain, he tried to make all the profit that he could by his consent, not allowing his women even to fetch a vessel of water for them from the river without stipulating before-hand for its price in beads; and, as their necessities increased, his demands became more exorbitant, so that they were reduced almost to a *beadless* state, and no one can say what might have happened if their stock had been entirely exhausted before succour could have reached them.

I sent down nearly all the small beads I had by the driver, so that they now had funds to support them for a short time; but the food they were able to purchase was of inferior quality (sour beer made of *upoko*,[1] a small worthless grain, was the only nourishment which I heard specified as having been obtained from the natives); and their courage and spirits had well nigh sunk to the lowest ebb.

The driver was visibly affected by what he had seen. His mind had

---

1. A species of millet (*Eleusine coracana*).

been gradually opening to receive religious impressions, and during our wanderings, I had frequent opportunities of instructing him, both in reading his native language, to which we devoted a little time every day, and in the principles of Christianity, which I imparted to him by word of mouth. In fact, he was so far a convert, that since the repetition of the Lord's Prayer, on the day of our departure, we had rarely missed using a short morning and evening prayer together; the *voorkist* being the homely altar at which we knelt; I, dictating the words from within the waggon, and he, following them from without.

A sermon which had been preached on Trinity Sunday, on the Gospel for the day, by my friend the Norwegian missionary, had impressed him more deeply than any teaching of mine, and pointed out to him the step which it was absolutely necessary for him to take, in order to obtain the grace which he sought. But he had never seen any one meet the approach of death, except with the terrible fear which the heathen must naturally feel; and he was surprised at the calm words of humble faith and hope which, during the quiet Sunday he had spent at Umgiba's, had fallen from the lips of an apparently dying man.

This one day's experience had at once given a deeper reality to the whole of the teaching he had received. His heart was full of sympathy and kindness, and he was most earnest to do whatever he could to help in this distress. I had a long talk with him as to the possibility of going down there myself, which I was most anxious to do, whatever the event might be. He was now well acquainted with the road and its difficulties, so after turning the matter over and over again, we resolved on the following plan:–

To move on that day to the next kraal, which was on the verge of the uninhabited wilderness; to sleep there, and to start the next morning at daybreak, and trek as far as the oxen could possibly go without being outspanned. The grass is so rank and unwholesome, that it is reckoned dangerous for cattle; they were therefore to be driven back at once to the kraal of Hluvunga,[2] from which we should have started in the morning, and there remain till further orders in charge of the leader, leaving the waggon in the *veldt*. Meanwhile I was to pursue my journey on foot, escorted by the driver. He did not think it possible that I could walk the whole way in one day, for I had no reputation as a pedestrian; it would

2. Unidentified.

therefore be necessary for me to sleep in the forest. This he assured me I could do with safety, as he could easily keep up a fire and watch beside me, and the lions have such an abundance of game, that they would not be tempted to attack us; on the contrary they would fear to approach. We could reach my brother without difficulty on the third day, and then I should be at hand to nurse him into strength if that were still possible, or, at any rate, to be with him if the worst should come. I might also try my eloquence on the surrounding natives, and persuade them to carry him through the wood. My driver had already tried to do so without success; but that was not enough to deter me; he was but a black man like themselves; but a white woman, a creature such as they had never yet seen − scarcely ever heard of − surely there was yet a chance that I might prevail! At any rate, God helping me, I would try.

It was settled then. I arranged to leave my two boys for the present, commending them to the care of my host, with whom I parted on pleasant terms.

I packed up a few *positive* necessaries − when it comes to a pinch, there are very few things that will stand that test. Some additional medicines and comforts for the invalids completed my store, which I was to carry in a leathern letter-bag over my shoulder, so as not to incommode me. My attendant would take such food as we should require, and a cloak for me to wrap myself in at night. I was quite ready for the morrow's expedition, and had no fears.

While we were talking, the men had been cooking a large potful of under-ground beans. I desired my driver to go and take his share; and then, for the first time since the tidings had reached me, I was alone.

I withdrew into my waggon. The weight that I had easily borne, while decision and action were necessary, fell crushingly upon me during this short interval of quiet.

I had full trust that I should be safe, and that I could accomplish, if it were still needed, the object of my enterprise; but what if I were too late? And then to go back to the Colony, or perhaps home to England to bear such tidings!

I threw myself upon the cartel, and tried to pray. No words would come but 'Help! Lord, help! for Thy Love's sake.'

This, and a burst of tears, somewhat relieved me, and by degrees I became more calm. I bathed by face, and came out from the waggon. It would never do at such a crisis for me to break down visibly, or lose my presence of mind.

I found that the men had finished their meal, and the leader was gone to fetch the oxen. While we were anxiously awaiting his return I was talking over my brother's state again with the driver, and hearing his account of the various symptoms which he had observed, when a young Scotchman,[3] respectably dressed, and wearing a red worsted comforter round his neck, approached the waggon and greeted me. I returned the salutation stiffly enough, I dare say, for my unwillingness to associate with the traders was very great, especially when I was travelling alone; but my friend, nothing daunted, proceeded to express his regret that Mr.— was in such trouble, adding, 'You are his sister, I presume?'

I could not deny this, and he then explained, that it was he who had left the letter on my *voorkist* the day before, and that he had received it from the Norwegian missionary, who knew him well, and who had told him of my hasty departure, and the alarm which occasioned it. He had also met the retreating party, and heard further particulars from them.

I told him the latest news I had received, and he inquired at once what I thought of doing? I stated my plan. He questioned whether I could carry it through. I answered I had every hope of doing so; that the divided journey would not be very trying, and that I had perfect confidence in my guide.

He said little more at the time; but told me that he had a cart and oxen a little further on, that he had just turned aside to see me, but was proceeding to Hluvunga's kraal, which lay in my way, and at which I intended to sleep that night. He hoped at any rate to see me again on my arrival there. So we parted, and my oxen coming up soon afterwards we inspanned, and moved slowly on.

Every step we took led us further from the advantages we had been enjoying, – wood, good grass, and clear water. We had a long, tiring day, and arrived late in the afternoon at Hluvunga's. He had two kraals which communicated with each other; the enclosure for the cattle was in the second, and I suppose served for both establishments.

As we drew near, I saw that there was a large fire outside the fence, with a noisy party of native men sitting round it; and I descried an encampment of waggons to the right, where a bush or two relieved the bare aspect of the country, and afforded a slight shelter from sun or wind, as the case might be. My waggon was drawn up nearly in front of the

3. Alexander Forbes was hunting with two relatives and W. H. D'Almaine (see next note).

gateway, by the side of the road or cattle track, by which we intended to journey on the morrow.

I had no sooner stopped than my friend of the red comforter came up and asked to speak to me. He said that, on reaching this place, he had met with two relations of his own, and another man[4] to whom my brother's name was well known; they had also a white driver with them, so that they mustered five white men altogether.

They had been holding a council with regard to my intended expedition, and, after talking over the matter carefully, they had agreed to request me to relinquish my purpose of walking down to Umgiba's, and to allow them to go in my stead.

I was overpowered with surprise and gratitude for this unexpected kindness, for it had never entered my head that any such help would be offered me.

At first I could not bear the thought of sitting quietly to wait; but my friend proceeded to explain to me in the kindest way that he and his companions were well acquainted with the country beyond the forest, and with the Amatonga, who differ much in character from the Zulus; that he had traded and hunted among them repeatedly, and had employed them to carry ivory; but that the difficulty of obtaining their help was considerable, and they might possibly have to take a day's journey or more beyond Umgiba's, in order to get bearers to convey the three sick persons, in case they should all be found unable to walk. In a word, he insisted that while they were well aware of the nature of the undertaking and could perform it, I should find difficulties in the way, of which I could scarcely form an idea. Lastly, he considerately reminded me that from the account I gave of my brother it was evident that he was still very ill, and would require nursing; and that if I finished my strength by the exertion of going to him, I should materially diminish my usefulness, and fail at the moment when I should be most needed.

I could not but agree to this, knowing that at best I had always more spirit than strength, and that though I might, and probably should, work on as long as the need lasted, yet it would be done at a fearful cost. So, after a little consideration, I agreed to accept this most kind proposal, which appeared to have come in answer to my prayer.

---

4. W. H. D'Almaine (1825–1885), a Zulu trader and farmer. This was his third hunting and trading trip to the Zulu kingdom.

The generous man persisted in disclaiming any thanks, saying they were only doing what they should expect others to do for them if a similar misfortune should befall them, as was not at all improbable in the course of their trading and shooting expeditions. I then asked if he would not take my servants. 'By no means,' he said; 'it would be desirable for me to have their protection and attendance, and he and his party had plenty of men of their own with whom they would prefer to work.' This was reasonable enough, and I knew it; for the great difficulty in dealing with the natives as servants is just this, that while they are perfectly obedient to their own master or mistress, they cannot understand a delegated authority, and will hardly recognise an order as proceeding from their employer if they have not heard it from his own mouth.

The groom had stayed with my brother, so I felt satisfied that he had a personal attendant to whose services he was accustomed, and who could understand him, while, for my own part, I was thankful to be left with my own people, and not to be entirely among strangers in this outlandish place.

I therefore begged my friend to convey to the rest of the party my grateful acceptance of their proposal, and to assure them that I was deeply sensible of their kindness.

One of them had a considerable knowledge of medicine, and carried a stock of drugs with him in his cart. I consulted him as to the symptoms from which my brother had lately been suffering, and for which I was not prepared with a remedy.

This he promised to supply; but declined to take any goods to satisfy the demands of Umgiba, saying that they could manage very well without them.

The conference being ended, my friends retired to their encampment, and soon after sent a message to ask if I had any meat with me. I answered in the negative, upon which I was presented with a leg of a gnu, which had been shot a day or two before. It was very good meat, something like beef; but without any fat. I was extremely thankful for it, as it enabled me to economise my flour, and besides, my men were hungry. The waggon of the friendly Scotchmen was always well provided with game, as they were expert marksmen. In fact, they kept me supplied during the whole of my sojourn at this place.

I sent my oxen back to Teu's, where I thought they would be safer, for Hluvunga's fence was not in first-rate order, and there was, as I have said before, neither good grass nor water in the neighbourhood.

There was no river at all, only a few pools in which the rain had been collected during the summer, and partly absorbed into the ground, so as to form an irregular kind of spring, which flowed a little in the morning, and was speedily diminished by the day's consumption. It was brackish and muddy, and I should think very unwholesome; but I have become accustomed to such water since that time by a residence of some years on the coast land of Natal, where these pools are frequent, and where drinkable water is a rare exception to the rule.

The party was off before daylight the next morning. I watched the figures in the grey dawn till one by one they sank below the hill and disappeared.

God speed them! They were gone upon a Christian errand. With what feelings should I see them return? Alas! who could tell? Only I must 'hope on, hope ever,' for to put the old proverb in a converse form, 'while there is hope there is life.'

I had received a promise, that in case it should be found necessary to delay the return, I should have some report of the state of the invalids, if a messenger could be found.

Accordingly, on the third day, my slave – 'Pig,' brought me a few lines, stating they were still living, and it was hoped they would do well; but that they could not yet be moved. A detachment of their rescuers had gone off to find bearers, and they would endeavour to complete their arrangements as soon as possible, but I must not expect them for a week.

No. I would only be thankful, not impatient; so far all was well.

Pig departed in high glee with his arm-rings and two extra presents, and I set to work to put everything in order. I had a grand day's washing, and ironed out my caps on the voorkist, beat and brushed the mattrasses, and made a comfortable bed for my brother in the waggon, imagining that we should be able, as soon as he arrived, to set forth on our homeward journey.

When all was ready, and there was nothing more to be done, I spent my time sitting or standing on the voorkist, straining my eyes over the distant plain.

With the aid of our telescope, I could see the whole tract of country, dotted with mimosa trees in some parts, and in others densely covered with them.

We had the advantage of being on an eminence, and it was a beautiful sight to watch the fleeting shadows of the clouds as they passed over the expanse below us. We could descry the forest beyond. It formed a long low line in the distance, and bounded our view in that direction.

To the extreme right was the gray wood, skirting the sea; and nearer to us, in a deep fertile valley, were herds of game of various kinds, and troops of quaggas.

These were in large numbers, and on scrutinizing them carefully with the glass, I could see them frisking and galloping about, and the little foals running up to their mothers and playing with them.

It was a curious peep into a wilder country than I had ever seen, and while the sight was in itself as beautiful as it was striking, it filled my mind with pleasant thoughts, and raised my heart in thankfulness towards Him, whose gracious love had made and cared for all the denizens of this teeming wilderness, and for ourselves had ordered in His Providence such an unlooked for deliverance in our extremity.

How many times during these days did I fix my eyes on some Euphorbia tree[5] or solitary thorn, and imagine it to be a group of figures approaching: 'Now surely they have reached the top of the hill! They must be here soon. Only look!'

An appeal to the sharp and practised eye of a native never failed to dispel my illusion; in fact, I found that my eyes were so dazzled and blinded with the glare, that they were no longer to be trusted. It was hard to refrain; but at last I made up my mind to desist from looking, and to endeavour to employ myself and await the event with patience.

---

5. The euphorbia or milkweed family of trees is very large; most are succulents, spiny and cactus-like, and contain a milky latex.

CHAPTER XI.

'And are ye sure the news is true,
And are ye sure he's weel?'
Nae luck aboot the House.

At length, about noon, on the seventh or eighth day, we suddenly heard a gun-shot. It was the signal of their approach! A few minutes afterwards we saw the file advancing over the hill. The sick men were carried in litters by the Amatonga, and their deliverers marched with loaded guns close by them, a host of retainers bringing up the rear.

The procession came slowly along, and halted in front of my waggon, where the bearers set down the two litters containing my brother and the boy. These two were to be my care, the other man was conveyed into one of the huts to be tended separately.

It was done, then! They had really brought him back to me!

I was so bewildered at first that I could hardly distinguish him from the boy who was a stranger to me. They were both disguised by an enormous bush of feathers, which had been stuck all over their hats to keep off the heat of the sun. My brother was very feeble, but knew me at once, and assured me of it in a faint voice.

I had no words to thank these good, kind men for what they had done. And they would scarcely hear what I did try to say, putting aside the whole matter as if it were just the simplest thing in the world to suspend their own employments and to walk thirty or forty miles in a burning sun to the rescue of a party of strangers.

I had a conference with the 'doctor' on the condition of the patients. He had found them all very ill, partly from exhaustion, and in some measure from the abuse of my strengthening remedies, the quinine and brandy, which they were unable to use with judgment in their very weak state. They had all passed the crisis of the fever, and were convalescent. Our business must now be to endeavour to restore their strength by the judicious administration of nourishment and medicines till we could venture to remove them further. At present it was entirely out of the question.

So I now knew what lay before me. Indeed I had deep cause to be thankful that the case was no worse. I had only to rise to meet the exigency, and this is never difficult. On the contrary, one's powers both of mind and body seem to increase under pressure, and one is surprised at the readiness of invention, as well as the physical vigour one discovers under such circumstances, which, if not evoked by an urgent call, would probably have lain dormant for ever.

I had only two patients on my hands, my brother and a boy of about sixteen — a slight, delicate lad at the best, and now quite blanched by his long confinement in the dark hut. Neither of them had strength to get in and out of the waggon; so I decided on pitching the tent in the sheltered corner made by the junction of the two kraal fences. The tent was round, with a canopy above, to which the curtains were attached by hooks, leaving two openings. The front was towards the north, so as to allow the sun to shine in, if we required its warmth; when the curtain was closed it was effectually shut out.

I put a mattrass on each side, and arranged a sleeping place, or rather a watching place, for myself across the back opening, at right angles to them. When we were all accommodated there remained but very little available space, so I still kept all my goods in the waggon, the few little things for constant use being placed in a box attached to the outer side of it.

I found my two charges very much in the condition of babies. They were not able to use their minds at all, and had forgotten most of the occurrences of the past month. My brother could not raise himself in his bed, and was in every way as helpless as an infant. The boy was led out into the sun for a little while every day, or laid in the shadow of the tent. He was also able to eat such food as we could procure for him.

My brother's state was far worse, as he could only swallow a little bread soaked in tea. The exertion of eating fatigued him, and solid food was too strong for his digestive powers. I made some beef-tea, or rather *gnu*-tea, for which the lean meat was well adapted; but a man soon tires

of slops, and our meat was too hard to be brought by any cooking to the requisite degree of tenderness without destroying its goodness altogether. One day the groom went out with my brother's gun, and, more by luck than cunning, shot a very large bird called by the natives an *Isémé*.[1] It weighed more than forty pounds, and it was as much as the successful hunter could do to carry it home on his back. I ascertained that the bird was considered very good eating; but it was rather hard.

A bright idea occurred to me. I remembered that a friend of mine in England had been recommended to give pounded mutton to her child when he was recovering from a dangerous illness, and he had been able to derive nourishment from it when meat in any other form was entirely forbidden. I thought I would try pounded *isémé*.

I accordingly summoned an attendant, and went with him into the kraal, where I inquired for the hut of the principal woman; I begged to speak with her, and when she appeared I requested her to lend me the stones with which she usually ground her corn.

She brought them out for me, after carefully ascertaining that I did not want to use them for any *umuti* or medicine, lest her stones should be poisoned. I then cut out some slices from the breast of the bird, and boiled them till they were sufficiently tender for my purpose, when I placed them on the broad flat stone, and pounded them with the large pebble till they were reduced to a soft mass. I stirred some of this into a little of the broth, boiled it up, and the result was some really palatable *isémé* panada![2] – a dish which would not be unworthy of a place on the dinner-table of the acclimatization society!

I regret extremely that I am unable to discover with any certainty the scientific name of this bird. I have searched in vain for it in the few volumes of African birds that have come within my reach. It is probably allied to the *Paauw*,[3] or wild Turkey, but is very much larger. I imagine it must be a kind of bustard.

Having thus made a new and successful experiment in the art of cooking under difficulties, I proceeded to vary the recipe with *gnu*; but it

1. *iSeme* is the Zulu name for both the Stanley's bustard (*Neotis denhami*) and Ludwig's bustard (*Neotis ludwigii*), which look similar.
2. Panada is either a dish made by boiling bread to a pulp in water and then flavouring it, or a thick binding sauce made from breadcrumbs or flour and seasoning. Spanish origin.
3. The Dutch word *pauw* actually refers to the bustard; see note 1 above.

was harder work to pound the meat, and though it made better soup, the panada was pronounced to be not so recherché as the first.

As our servants had not much to do beyond lifting my brother from one bed to another, for change, about twice in the day, and assisting me to cook and wash for him, they often went out with his gun to see what game they could kill.

The driver shot a fine fat gnu – it was a cow, and therefore likely to be tender. He left it on the spot, and hastened back to the kraal to fetch the women to carry home the meat. It was but a very short distance off, and they obeyed the summons with alacrity. When they reached the spot they found that the vultures had been there before them, and that, beginning from the bullet wound, they had laid open a considerable space, and had eaten away the flesh.

However, enough was brought home to serve for several meals for our servants, and to reward the bearers handsomely besides. There were a great many of them, for the creatures will never work, if they can help it, but in large parties, when the chattering they keep up is intolerable.[4]

Encouraged by his success on this occasion, the driver sallied forth again with the gun, and after walking some distance he fell in with a rhinoceros. He managed to get near enough to shoot at it; the animal, being hit, turned furiously on his enemy, who adroitly climbed up into a tree, and waited till it passed again within bullet range, when he contrived, with the other barrel, to inflict a wound somewhere about the neck. The monster then started off at his full speed, and made for the plain beyond.

When this story was related over the evening fire to the people at the kraal, they told the disappointed hunter that he need not have wasted his ammunition, for that the beast which he had encountered was not a common rhinoceros, but a man named Matikilala, who, for some private reasons of his own, or possibly through the malice of some powerful sorcerer, wandered about in this form; that his life was charmed, and no bullet could hurt him; and that after being shot at, he invariably trotted away to his relations in the far country beyond, and amused them with the tale of his day's adventures. 'The whole tribe,' said they, 'are probably laughing at you at this very moment.'

4. This is a further instance of Catherine's cultural prejudice. See Introduction, pp. (29)–(30).

What fun Matikilala could have found in coming out to be shot at, for the sole object of amusing his relations, it is not easy to divine!

The superstitions of these people are curious in the extreme. They fully believe in the power of the *takati*, or sorcerer. He is quite distinct from the *witch doctor*,[5] who is frequently employed to detect him – 'smell him out,' as they express it.

Every evil that can possibly happen to a person in body or goods is attributed either to the anger of the spirits of the dead, or to the machinations of these sorcerers. They are believed to have the power of preparing poison, of so subtle a nature, that if placed on the threshold of a house, it endangers the life of those who walk, or rather crawl over it. They are also supposed to poison food or snuff in such a manner, that if only taken once it brings on a slow consuming disease, from which nothing can ever save the sufferer. He may live for years; but die at last he must, and from that especial cause, and no other.

I once saw a young man, who had had a severe fever in his childhood, which left both his arms withered and useless. It was said that a *takati* had thrown a stick at him!

A woman who has called herself a Christian for many years, is persuaded that a chronic affection of the chest from which she suffers was produced by poisoned food. Her husband told me this himself, and I took the liberty to say that I thought he was disgracing his profession by entertaining such an idea; that if these men really possessed the supernatural powers attributed to them, they could only have acquired them in an unlawful manner, and that it was not for Christians to fear such open assaults of the enemy on their bodies, nor to seek to heathen doctors to remove their supposed effects.

It would be easy, if one were so disposed, to make a collection of curious stories from the lips of the natives as a 'pendant' to the volume of Maori traditions published by Sir George Grey.[6]

The old women tell the tales to their children, and so they pass on from generation to generation without much change.

Occasionally, however, some imaginative grandmamma will diverge from the usual routine and invent a new version, which becomes

5. In fact an *umthakathi* is a witchdoctor as distinct from a herbalist (*inyanga*).
6. See *British Museum catalogue of printed books . . . to 1955*, London, The Museum, 1961, v. 92, pp. 233–4 for a list of Grey's editions on Maori customs.

established among the hearers, and goes down to posterity side by side with the other.

I once had a servant, who, though he had been for some time a Christian, had a great regard for the curiosities of his own language and the old traditions of his countrymen. It was very amusing to hear him tell a story. I had some little native children under my charge, and they were often made the excuse for my own entertainment in this way. When he got into the vein, he would sit with his eyes fixed, and assume a peculiar intonation of voice, as if he were going through the most solemn proceeding in the world.

One story I remember particularly, which stands alone, and is unlike the usual run of the '*izinganekwana*,' or 'kinder-mährchen.'[7] I will give it entire for the reader's edification.

'In the old times there was a man who had a large herd of very fine cattle. They went out every day to graze in the plain, and a boy was sent to herd them.

'One day a troop of marauders from a distance came that way. They saw these fine cattle, surrounded them, and attempted to drive them off. They would not stir. The men clashed their spears against their shields, and made a great shouting to frighten them; but it was of no use, they quietly went on eating the grass as if nothing had happened.

'The robbers were vexed. They looked round about to see who had enchanted the cows. After searching a long time they found the herd-boy, who had hidden himself in a hole. They laid hands on him at once. "It is you, little vagabond, who have bewitched the cows. Come, drive them off directly, or we will kill you on the spot."

'The boy immediately began whistling to call the cattle together, and proceeded to sing:–

7. Legends, fables or fairy stories.

The whole herd set off immediately in the direction pointed out by the robbers, and after a long day's journey arrived at a large kraal which the boy had never seen. The cattle stood still at the gate till the boy, urged by the impatient men, had recourse to his song once more "Gi-li-li-li-li. Gi-li-li-li-li, the cows go in, li-li;" on which they rushed in at the narrow entrance of the enclosure, tumbling over each other in their eagerness to obey the word of command.

'The prize was surveyed by the robber chief, who was delighted with the acquisition, and singling out one of the finest and fattest of the oxen, desired that it should be slaughtered to provide a feast for his soldiers. No sooner said than done. The ox was adroitly stabbed in the vital part just behind the shoulder with a well-aimed blow that could not fail to cause instant death; but it would not die without the magical order! Neither would the skin come off, nor the bones submit to be divided; nor when put on the embers to broil, or boiled in a pot over a large fire, would one particle of the meat be cooked. It remained quite raw! The whole process, however, was in due time accomplished by the aid of the boy, who was then invited to share the feast, and had a portion of meat allotted to him, and plenty of beer. The latter he refused, and carefully secreted the meat, never touching a morsel. The rest of the party were in high spirits, they eat and drank plentifully, and towards the middle of the night they became overpowered with sleep.

'Not so the sharp boy. He watched in his dark corner till all was safe, and then gently rising, he slipped out of the hut and into the kraal, where he began his magic chant again, "Gi-li-li-li-li. Gi-li-li-li-li, the ox arises, li-li."

'And so it came to pass! The dead ox arose and stood before him alive and uninjured, and the boy drove his whole herd triumphantly away, and never slackened his speed till in the early dawn of the next morning he arrived at home, and delivered his charge unharmed to his master!'

I am not aware of any meaning attached to the words of the magic song; I believe they are no more than a Zulu equivalent to Fa-la-la, &c.

The legendary tales of the Zulus may be divided for the most part into two classes – those which serve simply for the entertainment of children, treating of ogres, and giants possessing great strength of body, but invariably deficient in mind, who are outwitted by a little clever fellow resembling Tom Thumb or Jack the Giant-killer. There are many of this type. The higher class consist of those which embody an old tradition or fragment of history. I am told that there is a story of a king who led his army through the sea, which divided before him, the waters rising on each side like a wall, and leaving him a dry passage to the opposite shore.

There are also others relating to the temporary concealment or degradation of some great personage, who submits to the indignity, and is finally discovered to be of royal if not of supernatural origin by the wonderful brightness of his skin, which shines like gold!

I have heard a very curious legend of this class, and though I do not exactly remember all its details, I give a sketch of it which may be interesting.

There was once a king, who, being in imminent danger of death by the violence of his enemies, or in some other extreme distress, sent his daughter alone into a far country (as I apprehend) to seek protection with a near relative of his own, who had a great kraal there.

The damsel (whose name I forget) departed on her errand, bearing a message or 'word' from her father. She passed the border of his dominions, and came into a land where she was not known. She journeyed on and on for many days. At length she met with an *Imbulu*,[8] a large reptile of the lizard tribe which lives in woods, and may frequently be heard crying in a monotonous and mournful voice. This creature is a chief actor in many of the Zulu stories.

The *Imbulu* said 'Good morning,' and inquired of the princess who she was, and whence she came.

She answered his questions without suspicion, and told him the name of the kraal to which she was bound.

'Do you know the way to that place?' said he.

'No; she would ask it as she went along.'

'I know the road perfectly,' said the creature. 'Indeed I am going there myself, and shall be happy to guide you.'

The girl was delighted with her new acquaintance, and they went on together. After a while the *Imbulu* said, 'I wish you would lend me your girdle.'

The princess complied; but was totally unconscious that with the

---

8. An iguana or leguaan, probably the rock leguaan or white-throated monitor (*Varanus exanthematicus albigularis*).

girdle she bestowed on the wily animal the power of assuming her shape. They walked and walked on till they arrived at her uncle's kraal.

The Imbulu at once introduced himself as the young princess, and told as much of her real story as suited his purpose (I believe the daughter was instructed by her father to remain with her uncle till further tidings should reach her). Having thus domiciled himself comfortably, he said to his adopted relations, 'I picked up that wretched girl upon the road,' pointing to the princess; 'you see how ugly and dirty she is! Her name is "Dog's Tail;" she can stay here if you will allow it, and make herself useful.'

The heroine, I suppose, found her lips sealed as if by enchantment, for it does not appear that she made any protest whatever. The hateful creature entered into all the privileges of a distinguished relative, while she, poor thing, was treated with every indignity. They made her work hard, and gave her the pots to lick, and were always taunting her with her *aristocratic* name of "Dog's Tail!"

The princess bore it all patiently, and did whatever she was bid. She was not allowed to go far from home lest she should run away; the Imbulu having given a hint to that effect.

At last the corn began to ripen, and required watching. The other girls did not like 'bird keeping,' so they set Dog's Tail to do it.

She went off alone to the gardens, which were, as usual, at some distance from the kraal, and not far from the river. She carried with her a small basket. This she set down in the middle of the field, and uttered a peculiar call, which had the effect of bringing all the birds of the neighbourhood together, and there they remained in a charmed state till it pleased her to release them.

The corn being effectually protected, the princess left her basket, and went down to the stream. She stood on the bank, and clapped her hands three times, when a goodly train of her own attendants arose out of the water, each having some article of her – well, we will say *'parure'*[9] rather than *clothing*.

They were followed by others loaded with food, and her father's whole herd of cattle brought up the rear. In fact she was surrounded by all the riches and state belonging to her real position.

9. French for a 'set of ornaments'. Catherine clearly feels that the word 'clothing' is an inappropriate description of an African girl's scant dress.

She bathed in the river, and washed off the mud with which she was covered, disclosing the regal brightness of her skin. She then donned her choicest ornaments, seated herself on the bank, and ate and drank her fill of the food to which she had so good a right. After enjoying herself thoroughly, and looking at her cattle (the chief occupation and amusement of a Zulu proprietor), she dismissed her retainers, who vanished as suddenly as they had appeared – the river closed over them, and they were gone.

She then took off and hid her ornaments, and carefully rubbed her body over with mud, and as the sun was about to set, she freed her feathered captives, and returned to the kraal as if nothing had happened.

From that time forward she continued during the bird-keeping season to carry on her daily amusement unnoticed, till one day by some chance or other she neglected to rub the mud over every part of her body as scrupulously as was her wont. A sleeping-place had been allotted to her in the hut of one of the grandmothers, and on this particular night, the old woman happening to awake, was startled to see something bright, which shone like gold, lying in the place occupied by "Dog's Tail."

She said nothing to the girl; but it is not to be supposed that she could keep such a matter to herself, and, by the time the sun was up, there was not a woman in the kraal but had heard the story. The stranger's wonderful success in bird-keeping had set them all on the *qui vive*, and they determined to watch her.

They began that very day; and, though baffled at first, they at length discovered how she spent her time.

They no longer wondered that she had grown so fat and comely on the licking of the pots! They questioned her closely as to her past history, and drew from her the whole truth.

The men were furious when it was repeated to them, and rushed to put a speedy end to the treacherous *Imbulu*; but it was not so easy a matter!

They eventually caught him and hacked him to pieces with an axe; but he turned himself into a pumpkin! They cut it up immediately, and cooked the whole of it; but they forgot that the seeds might contain the principle of life – and the Imbulu started up again!

After vainly attempting to destroy him, not without some injury to themselves, they resolved to lay a trap for him.

He was passionately fond of sour milk, and would eat any quantity of it. The men opened a large hole which had been dug in the cattle-kraal for preserving corn; it was about ten feet deep, and was now empty. Into this they poured all the milk they had, so that it was more than half full. They then told the Imbulu that they had a great treat for him. The greedy beast hastened eagerly to enjoy it, and tumbled into the hole, which was speedily filled up with earth and well rammed down; so there was an end of the persecutor!

The princess's affairs were settled at once – her followers gathered round her – she was re-instated in all her rights – and of course lived very happily ever afterwards.

The Imbulu of this and other stories is a remarkable creature, and the way in which he met his death affords us a slight link by which we may connect him with other monsters nearer home. The Worms, or Dragons, of the North of England resembled the Great Lizard of South Africa in their peculiar fondness for milk.

The 'Lambton Worm,' it is said, required the milk of 'nine kye' as his daily tribute. There is a Hindoo tradition of a serpent wallowing in a sea of milk. Yet one could scarcely venture to suppose a common origin to these chimeras from such distant parts of the earth.

While speculating on the subject of the Zulu stories, I would say a word as to their national songs.

They are, as a rule, monotonous and uninteresting; but the people sing in tune, and have a notion of harmony. It is a reproach to a man to say that he cannot sing a second. They keep time in the most correct and precise manner. Their howlings are often uncouth in the extreme, and the stamping of their feet and the motions of their bodies form no inappropriate accompaniment. The whole is simply disgusting.

Yet on one occasion when I was present at a native dance, given in my honour by a friend in Natal, I was much struck by the graceful movements of the men. They were about eighty in number, and they waved their shields to and fro, as by one consent, in perfect time to a low chant or song. It was a pleasing sight to see, until the women joined in with their awkward gestures and screaming voices, which entirely spoiled the effect.

There is a song which I frequently heard in the Zulu country, and remembered as being superior to all the rest. I have forgotten the words, if indeed I ever knew them. They contained a description of a raid of the Zulus on some other tribe, taking the cattle, destroying the kraals, &c.,

&c. I transcribe the melody, which I really think is worthy of a better and more interesting subject:–

CHAPTER XII.

'What if the lion in his rage I meet?
Oft in the dust I view his printed feet.'

———

'Soon shall this scrip its precious load resign,
Then what but tears and hunger shall be thine?'

COLLINS.

A DAY or two after the return of the party from Umgiba's my Scotch friend came to me, and told me that the Amatonga bearers were rested, and wished to depart, and that of course they must be paid for their trouble. Accordingly I went with him to the waggon to inspect my store of goods. I found that I had plenty of large beads and arm-rings, and a small quantity of salempore. The men had asked for cloaks to cover them, but my stock was far from sufficient to supply half their number. I think there were four-and-twenty of these bearers, eight to each litter. What was to be done? I could but give what I possessed, and suggested that the articles should be divided among them; but my friend was unwilling to disappoint the poor fellows. 'We have forced them to come with us,' he said, 'and there is no doubt that we can oblige them to accept whatever we choose to give: but they have wrought well, and deserve their reward. We may want their help for ourselves another year; we cannot vex them. Leave them to us, and we will settle the matter.'

And this I was constrained to do. I gave my piece of salempore; and whatever was wanting my kind friends supplied, refusing to take an equivalent of any kind, and protesting all the while that they were only doing it for their own interest!

This may perhaps seem to have been a trifle in itself; but to men who are daily exposing their lives, in order to accumulate a provision for themselves and those dearest to them, nothing is without its value. It was by no means a trifling act, and it is impossible that I can forget the delicacy and the generosity with which it was performed. I have never seen them again; but I rejoice to hear that they are prospering in the world, and I am sure they deserve it.

Our life in the tent, where we remained for a whole month, was quite regular and methodical, forming a decided contrast to the usual waggon life, with its variety of scenery and incident. To prepare and administer food — to change the position of the invalid, so as to relieve the soreness produced by lying so long upon a clay floor — to move him occasionally into the open air — these were my chief duties by day; while at night, if all went on well, I had only to warm a cup of tea for his refreshment, or perhaps to give him a little medicine.

Knowing that the fire must be kept up outside, I desired the groom to lie down just within the tent door, on the night of their arrival, that I might command his services; but the atmosphere was far too over-powering, and I felt that no trouble could inconvenience me so much as his presence. I therefore gave him his *congé* the next morning, to his great delight, for he was terribly frightened lest he also should take the fever. I knew it was useless to think of summoning him at night, for nothing short of an alarm of fire would have roused him; so I agreed with my driver, who slept in the outer kraal, that I would call him if I needed help. But I did not see the use of disturbing any one unnecessarily, and preferred being alone. I therefore managed for the most part to do the work myself. The fire-place, made up with a few stones, was about half-way between the hut and the waggon, and my little store of tea, sugar, and fresh milk (a treasure for which I bargained with Hluvunga) was kept in the side box, so that after kindling the embers I was obliged to go to the waggon for what I wanted. I was perfectly free and at my ease during this time, for the natives are terribly afraid of going out of their kraals after night-fall, when the wild beasts and still more dreaded sorcerers are likely to be abroad. I had always a provision of dry wood, and never during the whole month had occasion to summon my attendant but on two very damp nights, when a mist, or dew, resembling a fine rain, had so saturated my fuel that I could not possibly light the fire.

One night my patient was unusually restless, and I found it necessary to go two or three times to the waggon to get medicine or drink for him. It was very dark, and I could hear the short growl of the lions all around me. I observed also that there was a considerable stir among the cattle in the kraal – they were moving about uneasily, and knocking their horns together. This continued as long as I was awake, for I could not help dozing now and then. The next time I was roused I found that my part of the tent, which was near the fence, had almost fallen down; and it appeared in the morning that the pegs were loosened as if the ropes had been violently strained, though there had been no wind at all. I took but little notice of it, and had the pegs knocked in again.

By-and-by, as I was occupying myself outside the tent, the master of the kraal came up to me with something in his hand, and said, 'Look at this.'

I looked, and saw a clod of earth.

'What is there to see in that?' I asked.

'Do you not see the mark?' said Hluvunga.

I inspected it more narrowly, and saw some marks as of claws.

'It is a foot-print,' I observed. 'Is it a tiger's?'

'No,' said the man, putting on a very important face. 'It is he!'

He seemed afraid to mention the name of the king of beasts. There was no mistake. It was indeed his foot-print in the damp clay, and it had been found not far from my waggon in the very path which I had so repeatedly trodden during the dark night!

I have never consoled myself for not having met him; he would have been quite certain to run away, so I should have incurred no actual danger, but I should have been a heroine, which I have just missed! It was a great disappointment!

The men always declared the lion had passed over the ropes of the tent; but I would never believe it.

We spent, as I have said, a whole month at Hluvunga's. The boy recovered rapidly; but my brother suffered from ague, and was still very weak. However, it became absolutely necessary to move as soon as possible, for my three months' provision had already done duty for four, and the flour was fast coming to an end. We started, therefore, moving by slow and easy journeys, as my brother's strength could bear. We gave our last blanket to Teu, but it was not so good as I could have wished.

We carried some *gnu* meat with us, and a little buck or antelope, which we kept entirely for the chief invalid; the boy and I took our chance of such food as we could procure at the kraals. There was one whole day during which I could get nothing but a few grains of boiled mealies, and some thin cakes made of 'amahele'[1] meal, fried or baked in the pan, were reckoned for the time a great luxury among us; though my poor brother never tasted them without suffering for it afterwards.

Our arrangements for the night were now entirely reversed. My brother was obliged to sleep in the waggon. He was safer there from damp or unhealthy dews; besides, he could not bear the fatigue of moving, so we contrived always to outspan near some kraal, and to procure lodging in one of the houses for the boy and all the native servants. I, myself, spread a blanket on the ground beside the waggon, and, instead of undressing, put on some extra clothes before I lay down. I was thus alone and undisturbed, and within hearing of every moan or whisper of my charge.

In the daytime, the boy, whose head was yet too weak to bear exposure to the sun, sat inside the waggon, and I was promoted to the driving seat, from whence I could have a fair view of the interior without breathing the close atmosphere – the only thing that I really feared.

So we journeyed painfully on, and crossed the Umfolozi for the fourth and last time.

A day or two after this we passed a kraal at which we had been hospitably treated on a former occasion. Alas! the huts were burnt, or levelled to the ground, and an old decrepit woman was gathering sticks from the fence which had so lately enclosed a fine herd of cattle. We well knew the cause of this terrible desolation. On returning this way after parting with my brother, we had seen the soldiers at the gate, and heard that the owner of the kraal, who had been denounced to the king as an evil-doer, having been warned just in time, of the approach of the troop sent to murder him, had fled to hide himself in the neighbouring wood. The soldiers sought for him diligently, but in vain; and after they had given up the pursuit, he escaped by night, reached the Tugela, crossed into the British territory, and was safe.

His kraal was, of course, broken up; his younger women and children taken with the cattle to Nodivenga,[2] either to become the prey of the tyrant, or to be bestowed on his officers; the little ones to be brought up,

1. *Amahele* is probably a misprint for *amabele*.
2. Nodwengu; see ch. 5, n. 1.

until they reached an age at which they might be useful or saleable, according to their sex. The old women were left to vegetate on the spot as they might.

The state crime in most of these cases is the possession of a large herd, which excites the envy or cupidity of some powerful officer at court. If he has a grudge against any one it is easy to trump up a story of witchcraft or other misdemeanor, and the thing is done.

It was a piteous sight to see the wretched old women crawling about the ruins of their desolate home. *Such are the fruits of a despotic government*!

In our starving condition, the opportunity offered by my previous acquaintance with Umurulrulu, of the fertile country and the many cattle, was not to be overlooked. I sent the groom on to the kraal at dawn; he was an impudent fellow, but good natured, and sure to do this duty well.

This was the message I gave him:– 'Say to Umurulrulu, the princess is at hand, and she is hungry. The chief, her brother, has been at death's door, and is alive again, and he is hungry too. Tell the women to cook, and bring all the food they have to the waggon.'

Umurulrulu, I suppose, was impressed by the high tone I took, or perhaps he was in a liberal mood, for he obeyed the order implicitly; so that when we arrived, and outspanned in a pouring rain, in the road below the kraal, we saw a file descending the hill, each person bearing something on his head, with the exception of the master himself, who walked in front to convoy his offering.

There were bowls of sour milk, baskets of ground amabele and mealies, a large pot of fermented porridge (a very popular dish with the servants), pumpkin porridge; in fact, every delicacy of the season.

We had nothing to do but to eat and be satisfied – a feeling we had not known for many days.

Each of the bearers had something for his contribution, and the old fellow asked for a knife, a treasure which he easily obtained. This food gave us strength to proceed to the mission station,[3] where we halted for a few days to take rest and to be refreshed after our trying journey.

We were received in the kindest possible manner, and entertained as if we had been old friends. As our cattle were all with us, we killed a cow

3. See ch. 4, n. 19 and ch. 5, n. 10.

during our stay, that we might be provided with sustenance for the rest of the way.

The missionaries could not part with any flour, as their own stock was small; but a nice loaf and some fresh butter were the farewell gift to my brother, and no one can tell what store we set by it.

We were also fortunate enough to meet with a renowned African traveller, who presented us with a little tea, which was very acceptable. I had just come to the end of the small quantity I had obtained on the memorable day on which I purchased the goat, having eked it out by using pinches instead of spoonfuls.

Leaving the station, we passed through the Umlalazi district, where we found that considerable changes had taken place. The homestead of a native of high rank had been burnt to the ground, we supposed by accident, for the grass all around it appeared to have but lately sprung up, as if there had been an extensive fire. It probably became uncontrollable, as is often the case, and swept all before it.

We also saw a very large new kraal, which we did not recognise. On drawing up to it we found that old Nongalazi[4] had lately removed thither.

He was not at home, which I did not regret. We passed the night there, and on looking back after we had left it the next morning, we perceived that the inmates had set fire to the grass on which we had trodden, in order to prevent the danger of infection, so terribly do they fear the '*Imbo*,'[5] as they call the Zulu fever.

At the friendly kraal, which had served as our blanket depôt, we were welcomed with noisy demonstrations of joy. The report of our disasters had preceded us, and the people were delighted to see us alive.

Our trading Kafirs joined us, and we stayed two more nights to rest.

Here I was kept awake by the howling of the hyæna, incorrectly called the wolf. It would not have disturbed me so much had I not been lying on the ground, and imagined it might approach me. I do not think there was really the least chance of it, for they are skulking, cowardly creatures. I had heard them repeatedly, both in the Zulu country and in Natal, when sleeping in my waggon. At the Norwegian station they were so numerous and troublesome that it was found necessary to devise some

4. See ch. 4, n. 2.
5. Zulu for an epidemic or plague.

mode of destroying them, in order to preserve the sheep and goats. A small hut of wattle was erected in a convenient place, and the body of some dead animal was placed within it. A trap-door above the entrance was kept invitingly open, being held by a string fastened to the bait. The moment the hyæna entered and began to pull at the meat the door fell, and he found himself a prisoner.

During my stay the missionary caught several of these animals, and one morning two were found together in the trap. They were of different kinds. I conclude the larger one was the *Hyæna Cruenta*, the other one was probably *H. villosa*, called by the Dutch '*Strand Wolf*.'[6] I was told that several of their relations stood outside the trap, after the two were caught, howling and making a terrible noise. The native men said they were laughing at the ill fortune of their companions.

It happened that at the kraal at which we were now staying there was a doctor, not a witch doctor, but one skilled in herbs and charms.[7] He requested to be allowed to perform some of his quackery for our benefit. We did not oppose him, as we knew that whatever he wished to do was in reality intended as a preventive measure for his own friends and neighbours rather than to cure our invalids.

Having obtained our permission, he began by mixing and boiling some wonderful concoction in a pot, and when it was ready he dipped a grass broom into it, and sprinkled the waggon and all belonging to it, repeating some words, among which I distinctly remember, '*Puma, umtakati.*' 'Go out, evil doer.'

This was, I suppose, addressed either to the sickness itself, or to some supernatural agent who had brought it upon us. The doctor gave one of our men something which he declared to be a sovereign remedy against fever and dysentery. I believe it was the ashes of a plant which grows in the unhealthy district.

I was destined to have no rest at this place. The next night, or rather about two in the morning, there was a great stir which awoke me. I heard people calling one to another, and it seemed as if a party of men were setting out on a journey. At length the noise subsided, and in the morning I ascertained that the doctor and several others had gone to the sea for salt water to be used in some of their preparations. It was a long distance,

6. There are two species of hyaena in South Africa: *Hyaena brunnea*, the brown hyaena or strandwolf in Afrikaans, and *Crocuta crocuta*, the spotted hyaena.
7. See ch. 11, n. 5.

and they hoped by starting at this unseasonable hour to effect their return before the ensuing evening.

Just as we were ourselves preparing for our departure, we were surprised to see a native with a scarlet shirt.

We knew the livery well, and who it was that had thus kindly sent a messenger to seek us out. The man brought us a large packet, in which our friend had enclosed our English letters. This was a true token of our return to civilization. We had never received a line from home since we had left the colony, the arrival of the mails being in those days very irregular and uncertain.

What hopes and fears arose in quick succession as we opened our budget and saw the well-known handwriting of our own people! Setting aside private news, the letters were all on one subject – the Crimean war; the distress and privations endured by our brave troops, and the noble efforts that had been made to relieve them. The accounts were deeply and painfully interesting to us who now knew so well by experience the reality of hardships, though of course in a slighter degree than those of which we read.

How I longed for one of the ambulance litters in which the wounded were carried.

The shaking and jolting of an ox waggon are trying to a strong person; but for my poor invalid, whose weakness would scarcely allow him to sit up, it was very difficult to bear it patiently. No pillows that I could possibly arrange would remain in their places so as to relieve the grievous soreness, and it seemed hard-hearted to go on at all; while on the other hand, to rest or delay long without further advice and comfort would probably have been fatal.

Our letters from the colony were full of anxiety for our safety. A report of my brother's death had reached Maritzburg; and it was said that I, with the waggon and oxen, had disappeared altogether – no one knew what had become of me. The messenger had orders to inquire at the mission station, and to go on until he succeeded in tracing us out. Kind offers of oxen, servants, help of every description – proved that we were not forgotten, and that our friends were really desirous to do their best for us. Happily we needed nothing of the sort – good food was all we wanted.

We came to the house of which the young man (the third of the rescued party) was an inmate; he had already been brought home by the kind Scotchman. Here we obtained flour, mealie meal, and milk, which were all freely bestowed upon us. It was the same wherever we went, and it was with a strange mixed feeling that I literally begged my way home. No one would sell us anything: they insisted on giving us whatever we wanted.

Our good friends near the border, who had sent the messenger to seek us, were absent; but their house, and everything in it, was placed at our disposal. My brother could not be moved, but I went in and passed the night on a sofa, as I had done at the mission station. This was no slight refreshment, and enabled me to go through a tedious morning's work – that of settling with our servants. I had to pay them in cattle, and it was a new and difficult task to estimate their services, so as to allot the due reward to each of them. However, I got through it – perhaps without satisfying every one – and we then disbanded the troop of extra attendants, who had been hired for the expedition, retaining only the old servants who had lived with us before. The cattle were driven across the country by a shorter route, and we proceeded along the coast.

At the American mission station of the Umvoti[8] we were most hospitably received, and my brother enjoyed his *first night in a bed*! I was also permitted the same luxury. Our meal bags were replenished, and we carried off with us a most valuable present – as many oranges as we could stow away, and a whole bucket full of lemons. These I used to cool my brother's hands and face: it contributed greatly to revive him in the hot sultry days.

We met some friends at the Umhlali[9] who brought us out wine and food. It was like a triumphal procession. We were everywhere loaded with kindness, and hailed as if we had risen from the dead. My brother did not gain strength at all, and, having once enjoyed good accommodation, he dreaded more than ever to pass the weary nights on his hard mattrass in the waggon. It was on a Saturday afternoon that we found ourselves near the Tongati, where we hoped we might spend the Sunday in peace. We had still some little way to go, when a pouring rain came on and hastened the closing in of the evening. It now became very dark and slippery, and the oxen could make no way. Very unwillingly we turned

8. The Revd Aldin Grout established the Mvoti Mission Reserve after being expelled from the Zulu kingdom; see ch. 4, n. 14.
9. This may have been Capel Hanbury Williams who was Resident Magistrate for Tugela Division from 1853–1873/4.

aside to pass the night under a bush, still trusting, that if the weather cleared up next morning, we might reach a hospitable abode before the sun rose high. As soon as I had settled my patients I had my blanket spread under the shelter of the branches, and lay down to sleep; but in the middle of the night I was awakened by the rain dropping on my face. I groped my way to the waggon, under which I seated myself, gathering my blanket around me. Very soon the men, who had been also asleep, came from their different places to the same retreat, and there we all sat dripping till morning dawned.

We had picked up on the road a Kafir who had belonged to the shooting party. He had been left behind for some reason, so we took pity on him and let him come with us. He wore a coat of buck skins with the hair outward. It was a curious garment, but very serviceable, especially in wet weather. We were now close to the home of our leader. He begged leave to spend the Sunday with his friends, as we did not intend to move on; the man in the skin-coat undertook, in his stead, the task of herding the oxen.

The rain poured in torrents. It was as much as the men could do to light a fire. I was obliged to stand over it, sheltering it with my waterproof cloak, while they heaped on wood and blew the flame, till it had strength to burn without protection. Even then it would soon have been extinguished had they not set to work manfully, cut down stakes and boughs, and literally built a hut over the fire. It was so near the waggon that the canvas curtain in front could be fastened to some of the branches of which our temporary shelter was composed, and thus an awning was made, under which I was enabled to go from the hut to the waggon, to attend to my brother, without getting quite wet through.

On Monday the sky became again serene, and we made the best of our way onwards, and never rested again under a roof till we reached D'Urban: a whole month after our departure from Hluvunga's.

CONCLUSION.

MY tale is well-nigh ended. At D'Urban we met with the same kindness and consideration that had attended us ever since we returned to the colony. Two pretty rooms were given up to us for the night, and every comfort provided for us. We had then no acquaintance with the medical men of the town, and having determined to reach home as soon as possible, we were unwilling to enter upon anything that might cause delay. We were now happily in a place where we could purchase all that we needed; and having delivered the boy to his parents, I was relieved of any further care on his account.

The road was good, and the weather favourable, and we did not let the grass grow under our feet. We rose by starlight, and travelled while it was yet cool and pleasant. My brother suffered very much, so that I began to fear that he must be in a worse condition than we were aware of, and it became now my only object to see him at home, and at rest.

At length we reached Uys Doorns,[1] the next stage to Maritzburg, and here I slept in the veldt for the last time. We made up a large fire, and I lay down close to it; but I shivered with cold all night, and in the morning I found that not only the grass around me, but even the blanket in which I was wrapped, was sparkling with hoar frost! the first that we had seen during the whole winter. It was now the beginning of August. When we ascended the height, the Drakenberg was visible in the distance, white with snow!

About noon we drove into Maritzburg. I was seated on the *voorkist* beside the driver, while my brother lay in the waggon with the curtain down. It was as if we were bringing home a corpse.

However, we managed to settle him comfortably in the house, and he

---

1. Literally the thorns of Uys, the person to whom the land was first granted. It lay between Camperdown and Pietermaritzburg and the inn there was a regular halting place for travellers.

lay down to rest: thankful to be at home, but not very hopeful as to his ultimate recovery.

The next day was Sunday. I went to church, and returned thanks for 'having been brought out of great trouble.'

In those days, the cathedral being still unfinished, the service was held in the government schoolroom;[2] but it was so carefully and reverently performed that, with the essential part of Christian worship always present, one was tempted to forget the surroundings.

I certainly thought that my work was over for the time.

Our kind friend and physician[3] paid us a visit, and gave me a few directions; he said little: but he was not so much surprised as I, when, in the middle of the night, my brother was attacked by a seizure brought on by exhaustion. His life hung in the balance for many days, and was only saved, under God's providence, by consummate skill acting upon an originally sound constitution.

For two months more I watched by him night and day, until he gradually recovered, and regained his strength. It was a long trying time; and I think I could hardly have gone through it alone, but for the consolation that accompanied it.

The short intervals which I could spare from nursing my brother were claimed by our driver, who was also his constant attendant. His sick soul was turning to the only Healer, and needed the constant refreshment of holy words and prayer.

Before the invalid could walk across the room, the strong man had laid his burthen at the foot of the cross, and had received the precious gift of Baptism.

Thus two lives were at once granted to my prayers.

I have no more to say, except that I would thankfully go through all the trial again for such a blessed ending.

2. The foundation stone of St. Peter's Cathedral was laid in 1851 but the Cathedral was only opened in 1857. Until then services were held in the thatched schoolroom on the corner of Chapel and Longmarket Streets.
3. Unidentified.

SELECT LIST OF REFERENCES

ADLER, M., '"In a man's country": British women travellers in nineteenth-century South Africa', in *The societies of Southern Africa in the 19th and 20th centuries*, v. 19, London, University of London, Institute of Commonwealth Studies, 1992.

ARMSTRONG, W. A., 'The countryside' in *The Cambridge social history of Britain 1750–1950*, v. 1, edited by F. M. L. Thompson, Cambridge, University Press, 1990.

BALLARD, C., 'Traders, trekkers and colonists' in A. Duminy and B. Guest, eds., *Natal and Zululand from earliest times to 1910: a new history*, Pietermaritzburg, University of Natal Press, 1989.

[BARTER, Catherine (Charlotte)] *Alone among the Zulus: the narrative of a journey through the Zulu Country, South Africa*. By a Plain Woman. London, S.P.C.K., [1866?].

[BARTER, Catherine (Charlotte)] *Home in South Africa*. By a Plain Woman. London, S.P.C.K., [1867].

BARTER, Charles, *The dorp and the veld: or, six months in Natal*, London, Orr, 1852.

BRANFORD, J., *A dictionary of South African English*, new ed., Cape Town, Oxford University Press, 1980.

BROOKES, E. H. and WEBB, C. de B., *A history of Natal*, Pietermaritzburg, University of Natal Press, 1965.

BRYANT, A. T., *Olden times in Zululand and Natal*, London, Longmans, Green, 1929.

—— *A Zulu-English dictionary*, Pietermaritzburg, Davis & Sons, 1905.

—— *The Zulu people: as they were before the white man came*, Pietermaritzburg, Shuter and Shooter, 1949.

CALLAWAY, H., *Gender, culture and empire: European women in colonial Nigeria*, Houndmills, Basingstoke, Macmillan, 1987.

COLENBRANDER, P., 'The Zulu kingdom, 1828–79' in A. Duminy and B. Guest, eds., *Natal and Zululand from earliest times to 1910: a new history*, Pietermaritzburg, University of Natal Press, 1989.

COLENSO, J. W., *Ten weeks in Natal: a journal of a first tour of visitation among the colonists and Zulu kafirs of Natal*, Cambridge, Macmillan, 1855.

—— *Zulu-English dictionary*, 4th ed., Pietermaritzburg, Shuter and Shooter, [1905].

DELEGORGUE, A., *Travels in southern Africa*, v. 1, translated by F. Webb, introduced and indexed by S. J. Alexander amd C. de B. Webb, Durban, Killie Campbell Africana Library, 1990 (reprint of 1847 ed.)

DOKE, C. M., MALCOLM, D. McK., SIKAKANA, J. M. A. and VILAKAZI, B. W., *English-Zulu, Zulu-English dictionary*, Johannesburg, Witwatersrand University Press, 1990.

DUMINY, A. and GUEST, B., eds., *Natal and Zululand from earliest times to 1910: a new history*, Pietermaritzburg, University of Natal Press, 1989.

ETHERINGTON, N., 'Christianity and African society in nineteenth-century Natal' in A. Duminy and B. Guest, eds., *Natal and Zululand from earliest times to 1910: a new history*, Pietermaritzburg, University of Natal Press, 1989.

FEILDEN, E.W., *My African home; or, bush life in Natal when a young colony [1852–7]*, Durban, Griggs, 1973 (facsimile of London, Sampson Low, Marston, Searle & Rivington, 1887 ed.).

FOX, F.W. and NORWOOD YOUNG, M.E., *Food from the veld: edible wild plants of southern Africa botanically identified and described*, Johannesburg, Delta, 1982.

FYNN, H.F., *The diary*, edited by J.Stuart and D.McK.Malcolm, Pietermaritzburg, Shuter and Shooter, 1969.

HARRISON, J.F.C., *The early Victorians 1832–1851*, London, Weidenfeld and Nicolson, 1971.

HATTERSLEY, A.F., *The British settlement of Natal*, Cambridge, University Press, 1950.

—— '"Oxford collegian": Charles Barter', in *Oliver the spy, and others: a little gallery of South African portraits*, Cape Town, Maskew Miller, 1959.

—— *Pietermaritzburg panorama: a survey of one hundred years of an African city*, Pietermaritzburg, Shuter and Shooter, 1938.

—— *Portrait of a colony: the story of Natal*, Cambridge, University Press, 1940.

HOLDEN, W.C., *History of the Colony of Natal, South Africa*, London, Heylin, 1855.

HORN, P., *The rural world, 1780–1850: social change in the English countryside*, London, Hutchinson, 1980.

The James Stuart archive of recorded oral evidence relating to the history of the Zulu and neighbouring peoples, v.I–IV, edited by C.de B. Webb and J.B. Wright, Pietermaritzburg, University of Natal Press, 1976–1986.

KENNEDY, P.A., 'Mpande and the Zulu kingship', in *Journal of Natal and Zulu history*, IV, 1981.

MACLEAN, G.L., *Robert's birds of Southern Africa*, 5th ed., Cape Town, Trustees of the John Voelcker Bird Book Fund, 1984.

MIDDLETON, D., *Victorian lady travellers*, London, Routledge & Kegan Paul, 1965.

MOBERLY, C.A.E., *Dulce domum: George Moberly . . .; his family and friends*, London, John Murray, 1911.

OBELKEVICH, J., 'Religion' in *The Cambridge social history of Britain 1750–1950*, v.3, edited by F.M.L. Thompson, Cambridge, University Press, 1990.

POOLEY, E., *The complete field guide to trees of Natal, Zululand & Transkei*, Durban, Natal Flora Publications Trust, 1993.

PROCHASKA, F.K., 'Philanthropy' in *The Cambridge social history of Britain 1750–1950*, v.3, edited by F.M.L. Thompson, Cambridge, University Press, 1990.

RICKARD, C., 'Charles Barter: Natal diary, 14 August 1852 – 26 April 1853', edited with an introductory essay, place and personality index, B.A. Honours essay, University of Natal, Pietermaritzburg, 1975.

RUSSELL, G., *The history of old Durban, and reminiscences of an emigrant of 1850*, Durban, Davis & Sons, 1899.

SAMUELSON, R.C.A., *Long, long ago*, Durban, Knox, 1929.

SMITHERS, R. H. N., *The mammals of the southern African subregion*, Pretoria, University of Pretoria, 1983.

SPENCER, S. O'B., *British settlers in Natal, 1824–1857: a biographical register*, v. I-VI, Pietermaritzburg, University of Natal Press, 1981–1992.

STRUTHERS, R. B., *Hunting journal 1852–1856 in the Zulu kingdom and the Tsonga regions*, edited by P. L. Merrett and R. Butcher, Durban, Killie Campbell Africana Library, 1991.

SUTHERLAND, G., 'Education' in *The Cambridge social history of Britain 1750–1950*, v. 3, edited by F. M. L. Thompson, Cambridge, University Press, 1990.

THOMPSON, F. M. L., *The rise of respectable society: a social history of Victorian Britain 1830–1900*, London, Fontana, 1988.

WATT, J. M. and BREYER-BRANDWIJK, M. G., *The medicinal and poisonous plants of southern and eastern Africa*, 2nd ed., Edinburgh, Livingstone, 1962.

WRIGHT, J. and EDGECOMBE, R., 'Mpande kaSenzangakhona c. 1798–1872', in C. Saunders, ed., *Black leaders in southern African history*, London, Heinemann, 1979.

WRIGHT, J. and HAMILTON, C., 'Traditions and transformations: the Phongolo-Mzimkhulu region in the late eighteenth and early nineteenth centuries' in A. Duminy and B. Guest, eds., *Natal and Zululand from earliest times to 1910: a new history*, Pietermaritzburg, University of Natal Press, 1989.

INDEX

Numbers in brackets refer to the Introduction. The text of *Alone among the Zulus* is numbered 1–106.